THE SYSTEM

THE SYSTEM

*Who Owns the Internet, and
How It Owns Us*

James Ball

BLOOMSBURY PUBLISHING
LONDON • OXFORD • NEW YORK • NEW DELHI • SYDNEY

BLOOMSBURY PUBLISHING
Bloomsbury Publishing Plc
50 Bedford Square, London, WC1B 3DP, UK

BLOOMSBURY, BLOOMSBURY PUBLISHING and the Diana logo are trademarks
of Bloomsbury Publishing Plc

First published in Great Britain 2020

A catalogue record for this book is available from the British Library

ISBN: HB: 978-1-5266-0724-9; TPB: 978-1-5266-0725-6; EBOOK: 978-1-5266-0721-8

2 4 6 8 10 9 7 5 3 1

Typeset by Newgen KnowledgeWorks Pvt. Ltd., Chennai, India
Printed and bound in Great Britain by CPI Group (UK) Ltd, Croydon CR0 4YY

MIX
Paper from
responsible sources
FSC® C020471

To find out more about our authors and books visit www.bloomsbury.com
and sign up for our newsletters

For our future overlords

CONTENTS

Introduction

THE INTERNET WAS supposed to be a thing of revolution.

From the first days of coming to the public's attention, it was connected to a certain type of counter-culture – to cypherpunks and hackers, people learning, exploring and challenging authority. As early as the 1990s there was a declaration of online independence, telling the powers that be in the old world to stay away. A new order would surely emerge.

Even when business came to the internet world, it was going to be different. The reach and scale of the internet would enable a 'long tail' of small and independent producers to flourish. Online companies were launched talking in earnest terms of changing the world, with 'don't be evil' mantras alongside – and generous share options making even their office decorators rich.

For a long time, you could convince yourself it was all the real deal. At the start of the last decade, WikiLeaks used its unique online platform to challenge the world's biggest superpower with an unprecedented series of leaks. Shortly afterwards, the world's biggest social media companies were credited with boosting Arab Spring protests against corrupt and dictatorial governments.

Such was the mood towards the internet that the exultant opening ceremony to the 2012 London Olympics culminated in a seventeen-minute dance sequence celebrating Tim Berners-Lee for creating the World Wide Web and giving it to the world for free. Berners-Lee himself featured, tweeting the words 'This

1

is for everyone' as they simultaneously appeared in lights across the stadium. The internet was almost indisputably a thing to be celebrated.

That's not the spirit of the world at the start of a new decade. The internet giants are viewed with mistrust, accused of playing a role in spreading misinformation, enforcing censorship and avoiding tax. Its billionaires are scrutinised and condemned for their working practices. Residents around the palaces of Silicon Valley have come to resent their corporate neighbours.

Has the internet and the people running it changed so much in such a short time? Did we get them wrong all along? Or is the problem with what we suspect they've been up to?

One thing, at least, is clear. The world's biggest technology companies are now the world's biggest companies full stop – and they are not ready for the scrutiny that goes along with that. From being hailed as 'disruptors' and the good guys shaking up the system, they have suddenly discovered they *are* the system.

The easy route – and the conventional wisdom – is to say that the dream has gone bad, that an engine of tremendous potential has been wasted. That story says also says the dream can be reclaimed: the internet is still inherently a force for good, a democratising power.

It's a story that needs a villain, and there are no shortages of candidates on offer: the bosses of the technology giants, the agents of Russia's intelligence agencies, dictators and party bosses across the Middle East and into the Great Wall of China, whoever. These people are standing in the way of the dream – move them and the internet's disruptive power for good will be restored.

It's a tempting story. It's a story many armchair pundits want to tell. But it's not the story of this book.

INTRODUCTION

Whether they are loved or loathed, the four companies we always talk about when we talk about 'the internet' – Amazon, Apple, Facebook and Google (now formally known as Alphabet) – are not the internet itself. They are products of the internet, engines running along the railway lines set out by the internet's very structure.

Despite its lofty language – the use of words like the 'cloud', language which suggests something free and natural, beyond the control of people – the internet is a network of physical cables and connections. It's a web of wires enmeshing the world, connecting huge data centres to one another and to us, storing and sharing the innermost details of our lives.

Each of those cables is owned by someone, as is each of those data centres – and every piece of that data is also owned by someone, and that someone is almost never the person who that data is about. In turn, each of those owners was backed and financed by someone, and each physical site lies in the jurisdiction of a government and a myriad of regulators. We refer to the online world as if it's abstract from the reality we all occupy every day: this is a myth, and it's a myth that obscures where the real power lies.

Online power is offline power: the internet has handed more power, control and money to the people who already had plenty. It may have changed the people in one or two seats at the top table, but it has not changed the system itself in any ways that matter.

Systems don't build themselves. The internet and the way it works were all human decisions, made by groups of men – it's almost always men – in small rooms, with their own particular ideologies, motivations and divisions. This book aims to take you into those rooms, to meet those men, to find out why they made the decisions they did, and what the consequences were for them, and for us. Not all of them are household names, but each of them has helped shape the internet, and the world the internet has shaped, in profound ways.

The internet is fundamentally hard to think about and hard to understand, despite the fact that more than three billion of us use it in some form every day. What do we even mean when we talk about 'the internet'? Do we mean the World Wide Web, what we see from our browser? Do we include the banking networks that now operate online, between businesses, almost every time we buy something? Do we mean the complex series of rules and protocols that govern flows of data across the world? Do we mean the business model behind it all, joining and auctioning our data, thousands of times a day, always out of our sight?

Most of these issues aren't in our daily thoughts, and often seem too technical to be worth understanding. But it's these things that shape the real internet – the big four tech giants are products of all of these factors.

Looking into the architecture of the internet – who built it, who governs it, how it works, and who funds it – becomes, then, a way of looking at the real power structure of a huge swathe of the modern world. While we might think of Mark Zuckerberg, Larry Page, Jeff Bezos or the other charismatic dotcom CEOs as the new rulers of the world, they're just the tip of an iceberg. It's time to see what lies beneath.

I am at my very core a creature of the internet. My earliest childhood had computers hooked up via creaking modems to the bulletin boards that were the precursor of the popular web.

As an adult, my childhood obsession had metamorphosed into using the internet, and working to chronicle it – as a tech journalist, as a WikiLeaks staffer, as someone later working on the NSA (National Security Agency) leaks from Edward Snowden, who documented how the intelligence agencies dominated the networks that had felt like my home.

INTRODUCTION

A decade or more of reporting on the internet takes you across the world – from south London squats full of idealistic hackers, to secure operations rooms. For this book, I have tried to get inside the closed rooms, to meet the people who've made the decisions that have shaped the internet and to hold them to account. I've tracked down people in cluttered academic offices, in corporate penthouses, in electromagnetically shielded secure rooms from which no signals can enter or leave. The result, I hope, offers us a chance to meet and to confront the power brokers, the money men and more who are usually well beyond our view.

When it comes to the internet, there is a truth we need to acknowledge early: this story is overwhelmingly Western, and overwhelmingly male. Trying to tell the story without noting this fact – and, as we go, noting the effects of this homogeneity in missing some of the mistakes on the path – would be to tell the story badly.

THIS IS A book of three parts. If you're going to understand the system, you need to understand its components and their mechanics. Part one covers these chapters, explaining the history and structure of the internet and its power dynamics (and on the technical side, there's a glossary if you need reminders of any specialist terms you encounter – jargon has been kept to a minimum and you're not expected to pick up this book knowing any of it).

It opens with the architects of the internet, its earliest pioneers. While the internet has recently turned fifty years old, most of its founders still live, and for the first thirty years of its life it was a niche concern, to be left to the nerds – and yet in this largely unscrutinised phase, almost all of the key decisions and protocols used to this day were formed. It's also here that we discover the free-wheeling idea of the internet isn't quite what it seems, that it was always a lot closer to government and the establishment than its image might suggest.

The next chapter turns to the cable guys: the people who own and operate the cables that make up the physical internet itself – we might think of the cable companies as just the annoying people who send us a bill each month and try to upsell us, but they play a much bigger role as a power broker behind the scenes, and often clash with the far more visible online companies we hear about each day.

This section closes with the custodians who actually run the core mechanics of the internet. When you type in a web address, do you know who's in charge of deciding which computer – out of the billions on the network – you're asking to be connected to? Who's in charge of that address book, and how does it work? And who decides which one of the many different routes of cables will take you there – who runs the internet's satnav? The answer is a surprisingly fascinating one – but given how critical the internet is as a part of the world's infrastructure, a disturbing one too.

But the physical infrastructure is only half the story. Beyond the cables, the companies and the governments there is one more power in the online world – **the money men**. The driving force behind almost every household name in the tech world is venture capital, a business model based on dropping millions of dollars into companies in the hope that they will grow exponentially fast, and then sell for hundreds of millions, if not billions. But anyone putting in millions expects to get it back tenfold – and that drives many of the decisions we see tech CEOs make, day in and day out.

The way those CEOs tend to build the businesses their funders want is via **the ad men**, the people responsible for targeting and tracking you in thousands of ways on the internet every day. The man who invented programmatic advertising – the ads supposedly aimed precisely at you on almost every website you visit – reveals the method by which his industry scatters your personal data across the internet, further than you would ever imagine, in what even he admits is a disaster.

In part three comes the melee. The internet is a constant battlefield. This can range from its role as the front line of the culture wars, to confrontations between superpowers, through cyber attacks and information warfare. It spans the battles between global tech giants and the countries and agencies which would check their power, as well as the resistance to the very idea of a corporate internet.

As light travels down the fibre-optic cables which cross the Atlantic and the world's other oceans, intelligence agencies split it, siphoning it off and examining its data. The cyber warriors of the planet have a duty to protect us online, but also to spy on adversaries, a dual role and a tension which has left us all vulnerable. Through the Snowden leaks and a trip to the front lines of the cyberwar – thousands of state versus state daily hacks impacting on all of us – the hidden conflicts of the internet will be seen in plain sight.

And finally, we come to the rulemakers, the regulators who are supposed to be actually governing this mess, and the resistance: activist groups trying to hold the internet's power in check – a shift from glitzy multimillion-dollar offices to leaseholds next to garages and one-man operations, a sign of the inequality of the fight they face, yet still score frequent triumphs.

Although this book might be a bid to reveal the systems behind the internet, it's fundamentally a human story, told through the people who have made the decisions and the people who have been affected by them.

A MOMENT, THOUGH: if the internet is less a concept than a collection of infrastructure, cables, rules and regulators, is it really anything more than a tool? If it's a tool, it's tempting to believe that its potential for good or ill lies solely with who's wielding it. A hammer can be used to build a house or break into one, and can be blamed for neither. The internet, surely, must be similarly intrinsically neutral.

We have to remember that new tools – even ones on a far smaller scale than the internet – can reshape the world, with seismic consequences felt across decades, if not centuries.

If we want to think of how a tool can reinvent the world, we need look no further than the invention of the railways and the steam trains to run upon them. In the nineteenth century, railways were a communications technology – at the very least, they connected the world in a way that was faster and more reliable than before. They boosted the potential for efficiency, and they became integral to the business models of numerous other industries. And because not everyone could easily start a railway – all that track, not to mention the labour to lay it, doesn't come cheap – the industry quickly became dominated by a few giant players and their financiers.

These things can similarly be said for the architecture of the internet: just as railways could be used to create new monopolies in other industries – by charging different rates to different companies, or playing favourites – so too can the internet.

The internet, left unchecked, is a monopoly-making machine, an engine designed to concentrate power, attention and more in the hands of those who already have it.[1]

This was the potential of the railways, too – and the reason we don't live in the second century of a gilded era of monopolies in every industry is not thanks to the benevolence or wisdom of the people who built and owned the railways. It's because we took deliberate political and legal actions to stop them, in a series of vicious political and social battles that took decades.

That required building whole new branches of law, it required huge political will and it required some dramatic showdowns.

8

INTRODUCTION

It took nerve. But when an invention truly changes the world, that's what needs to happen next.

More than a century ago, a handful of wealthy and well-connected men seized on the inventions of others – some themselves would-be entrepreneurs, some well-intentioned naïfs – and used them, with their wealth, to build the industrial era and leverage its huge financial returns for themselves.

The consequences of what those men did – in what is sometimes referred to since as the 'Gilded Age' – were calamitous, fostering resentment among millions of struggling masses against an increasingly rich elite, sowing the seeds for populism in the twentieth century, and through industrial technological change and political pressure, fuelling in different ways both of the twentieth century's world wars.

The parallels could hardly be clearer: we are once again seeing a technological revolution, benefiting a new elite and their old-money financial backers, until recently with the enthusiastic support of most lawmakers and regulators. And by telling us all that the whole thing is too boring and complicated for us to understand – it's code, it's algorithms, it's machine learning, it's AI, they say – they've stymied our questions.

The early consequences are the same, too. Across the developed world, the share of wealth held by the very richest is increasing to the highest it's been in decades.[2,3] Globally, a populist backlash is rising, with far-right and anti-establishment parties and movements doing better than they have for decades.

These are the stakes in play: working out how to shape and control the internet means working out how to shape and, to an extent, control the world.

We need to figure out how to harness it as something which works for all of us, in the way that we managed to at least partially harness the potential of the industrial era to work for humanity as a whole: enriching us, giving us more to eat, easier housework, travel and more, and averting the disastrous backlashes to gross inequality we have seen in the past.

The first step of this is seeing the system as it really is. This book is an effort to do exactly that, to tell the story of how the internet came about and how it works.

Part One

THE MECHANICS

1

The Architects

ON THE EVENING of 29 October 1969, a group of men gathered in a room at the University of California, Los Angeles (UCLA), to do the first ever test of a potentially world-changing new creation: to send the first message over what would become the internet.

At the time, no one was envisaging the global network we think of today. Instead, this was a test of a much more modest proposal – funded by the US Department of Defense (DoD) – to connect together room-sized computers at four academic institutions, so that people in one could log in to the computer at another. This would enable them to use computers remotely if, for instance, their own was being used or they needed to do some specialist task their own hugely expensive computer could not accomplish.

Three years into the project, the academics, postgrad students and contractors had completed their first connection, between UCLA and Stanford Research Institute (SRI). Instead of any kind of grand launch, those involved with the project gathered at each end of the connection to see if their computers would talk.

The two institutions were joined with a 50 Kilobits per second connection – a connection around 1/374th the speed of an average modern US broadband account.[1] They decided the first thing to do was just use the technology as it was intended, to log in to the other computer remotely. Professor Leonard Kleinrock,[2] UCLA's head of the project, later recalled how researchers at both ends of the communication were simply trying to send and receive the simple command: 'login'.

'We had Charley Kline at our end, we had Bill Duvall up at SRI. And just to make sure this thing worked, they had a telephone connection. Now the irony here is just dripping. We were using a telephone to prove our [technology] which is about to displace the telephone network, so they could communicate.

'The point is Charley typed the L, and he asked, "Will you get the L?"

'Came back, got the L. Charley typed the O. "Get the O?"

' "Got the O."

'Charley typed the G. What happened? Crash.'

The very first message on the internet crashed the computer of its recipient – perhaps something of an inauspicious start. But in the spirit of its early serendipity, one that also resulted in a pleasing story.

'The very first message on the net,' Kleinrock notes, 'was "LO", as in "lo and behold".'

Though the transmission resulted in a crash, the overall idea had worked: at least some of the data had been transmitted and received successfully. The error had been the result of well-intentioned efficient coders, making their computer transmit the rest of 'login' – the 'g-i-n' – once it realised that was the only command the user could be typing. The network transmitted that, but it was more than the receiving computer expected, and caused a crash.

While it might not look good, that was the network working as intended – in theory, at least. After around an hour of hasty recoding, the researchers were ready to try again, and this time the full 'login' message was sent.

The internet was off to a start, even if it was an awkward one.

THE ARCHITECTS

ONE OF THE men in the room at that very first test of the internet was Steve Crocker. I meet him, now a sprightly man in his seventies with close-cropped grey hair, in Bethesda, a small town in south Maryland, not far from Washington DC. He elects to meet in La Madeleine, a chain 'French bistro' down the road from the offices of Shinkuro, his online research and development company.

Over filter coffee, we talk about Crocker's life and career. He has the eye for detail, bordering on pedantry – he doesn't tolerate any inaccurate or sloppy phrasing – of the trained software engineer, tempered by a friendly and easy manner, an enjoyment of a chance to tell some of his stories. He has plenty of them to tell.

As part of the team who built the first precursor to the internet, Crocker helped set the rules, working to build some of the protocols that power the internet – and how it is governed – to this day.

He's in the 'Internet Hall of Fame',[3] one of a small group of its 'pioneers' – the handful of graduate students who built the internet (the most famous of whom, Vint Cerf, still works for Google as its 'chief internet evangelist').[4] Crocker went on to serve as the chair of the body which governs the way the internet handles how web addresses work, and has had senior roles overseeing the security of some its core networks.

As Crocker tells it, the story of the internet's earliest days isn't quite the free-spirited, revolutionary tale that some might imagine.

One version of the story says the internet grew out of the need for universities to get access to computing power to further their research. Another maintains that the internet was a by-product of the Department of Defense looking for a way to make sure its nuclear deterrent would work even if its communications were disrupted.

Neither story involves anyone far-sightedly imagining they were building a global network that would change the planet. For the academics, the birth of the internet came as a byproduct of fixing a much more mundane problem: universities weren't making efficient enough use of their expensive computers.

THE COMPUTERS OF the mid-to-late 1960s were gigantic affairs well beyond the reach of any kind of regular user. Transistor-powered machines were only just starting to be replaced by computers with integrated circuit boards – something you now find in every toaster, let alone every computer, but then the cutting edge of technology. And this vast expense meant that the institutions that had invested in these kinds of computers needed to maximise the use they got from them.

Initially, the answer that institutions – which used the computers for advanced physics, maths and other research – hit upon was to keep waiting for computer time in a kind of queue. Known as 'batch processing', people would leave their task – their code or instructions – for the computer in a queue that could be hours or days long, and come back for their results later.

In modern terms, this is a little bit like typing a Google query and getting the response back perhaps twelve to fourteen hours later, and then if you see a site you want to visit on the results list, waiting another twelve to fourteen hours to get there. In practice, the computers were being used to calculate formulae or run simulations, so if you'd made some error in your instructions that made the output gibberish you would have to hope for better results next time you were at the front of the line.

For the researchers, the problems of batch processing were many and deeply frustrating; but computer processing time was worth far more than the time of graduate students. Using a computer like we do now, sitting at the keyboard and entering instructions in real time, could leave machines idle when the user thought or was distracted. Given how expensive and rare computers were, that wasn't an option.

The problem then was finding a way to keep a computer busy while also trying to help it be 'interactive' – responsive in something more like real time, rather than hours or days later. Computers were, like holiday homes, big and expensive, and no one person needed to use one all the time – so why not set it up so they would be used as timeshares?

Multiple people could have access to a computer at once, via multiple keyboards, and it would process each instruction in sequence. People would still have to wait, but for less time, and it wouldn't matter if each person wasn't constantly requiring it to work at 100 per cent.

This idea became part of computer history lore – at least among hardcore nerds – thanks to 'the mother of all demos', which had taken place almost fifty years to the day before Crocker and I had our conversation. It happened on 9 December 1968 in San Francisco, and it became the model for every dramatic product reveal demonstration that has followed ever since.

'This was Doug Engelbart's laboratory at SRI, where he introduced the mouse, hypertext and graphics to a major meeting,' says Crocker.

Today all of those elements seem mundane, but this was an era when instructions for computers were still often entered via punch cards. Seeing a mouse work real time to shift a pointer on a graphical computer was revolutionary.

But Engelbart's vision went further than that: he had set up a dozen such terminals connected to the same computer, which gave a bit of its time to each one as needed, with the intention of making the system interactive.[5] And since multiple people can work on the same computer at the same time, why not try to make it easier for them to work together?

Many of the elements highlighted in Engelbart's demonstration would take decades to come to fruition, but his showy demonstration drew real attention to the potential of time-sharing – and how it could so obviously be taken further: if sharing time on one computer worked, and helped collaboration, doing so on multiple machines would very obviously take it further.

'You had these time-sharing systems and you had these laboratories that people were doing advanced research in,' Crocker says. 'In that environment, the people who were running those said, "We're going to connect our centres together and that will be a big leap forward with respect to networking. It will be a big leap forward with respect to just building our research community." That's what led to the ARPANET project.'

The ARPANET project was the network which became the internet, and was even with its more modest origins a wholly new idea for how to network computers.

Limited networks, a term for any system which connects up separate computers, were not unheard-of at the time – airline reservation systems, for example, might join up a few computers in a very specialised way, as might some advanced military command and control systems. But each network would work in its own bespoke way, with its own bespoke protocols and set-up, effectively speaking entirely different languages which no other network could speak, and each network would only work for one very specific task.

This was no good for the creative research universities needed – they required a network that would do a variety of different tasks, including some perhaps not even thought of when the system was designed. What they needed instead was something much broader, a network that could send or receive *any* kind of data.

Working out how to create something more general was a new problem. How could you send and receive data efficiently?

How could you make interaction possible? How could you make sure what was sent and received was consistent if you got interference on the line? These were just a few of the intricate and often highly technical complications the idea of a generalised network raised. For most of us, they sound like a headache. To a research community, they sound like fun. And to the US Defense Department's still freshly minted Advanced Research Projects Agency (ARPA), it sounded like an opportunity.

ARPA'S DECISION TO fund the project proved seismic to the fabric of the internet in a number of ways, some of which were obvious at the time, but some of which are still barely noticed – but does mean that from the get-go, the internet was not just a university invention, but also one intricately tied up to the US government, its military and the needs of the Cold War, even if it wasn't regarded as a tightly held official secret.

In reality, Crocker says, the atmosphere was quite relaxed: networking the computers of four research universities was an interesting project, but hardly an earth-shattering one. The senior faculty concerned had agreed the overall aims, and looked forward to seeing how it might aid their research when done, and then were happy to leave the details to their graduate students to thrash out among themselves.

Those graduate students became the so-called fathers of the internet.

'The small task of how you got to actually hook things up and make it work was delegated down to the kids,' Crocker explains. 'You have the project heads at each of these sites who had agendas for their own research. They have their core research projects and they were in their careers and pushing along their research which was being funded ... and now you have this sort of added task that is just imposed on them. This router is going to be delivered to your laboratory – you have to connect up your computers to them. All right, well, we'll get this kit over here. It wasn't quite as crude as that, but it had that flavour.'

The universities had agreed they wanted a network that could make it possible to do two things: to send and receive files between different computers, but also to make it possible to log in remotely to a computer at another institution, and to then give that computer instructions.

The two goals were, to an extent, in conflict with each other – based on the logic at the time, you would build networks differently to best suit one or the other. To build one doing both left a lot of details to work out, so the institutions had a meeting – the very beginning of the internet.

'In August '68 representatives from the first four sides were called together to meet each other and get going on this,' says Crocker. 'We were not the heads of the projects we were working on, we were staff or grad students from whatever. As it happens, Vint Cerf and I were both at UCLA and we went to that first meeting. SRI and Santa Barbara and Utah all sent representatives and a few other onlookers – call it a dozen people. The person who organised the meeting came with some notes about what we might think about. We said, that's fine, but we wanted to think about a more general framework, because we could see that if we went through all the trouble to build the software that would make it go, you'd want to use it for a lot more complicated things.'

ARPA was the sole funder of this early era of the internet – it had first secured $1 million of its internal budget to study networking in 1965, supposedly diverted from its ballistic missile programme after a persuasive twenty-minute pitch to its then director, Charles Herzfeld.[6]

The availability of this funding helped shape the early internet: the time and energies of the graduate students across the institutions had been paid for, giving them some latitude to experiment. Had universities been guardedly watching what was coming from whose budget, the scope might have been curtailed far earlier; this way, the team had the chance to try a few things, work collaboratively, and more.

'None of us needed to charge,' says Crocker. 'With all of us, our time was paid for, our facilities were paid for. We weren't in competition with each other. There wasn't any commercial pressure, so it was natural. It turned out to be extraordinarily fortunate because it had a dramatic effect in terms of spurring the participation of other people down the line.'

In traditional communications networks – like the landline phones of the time – huge quantities of effort and engineering went to tracking billing. Who was liable for a connection? How long was it? At what rate should it be charged? As ARPANET was initially funded by government, this billing requirement wasn't built in.

This, and other factors, helped shape the decision to build a network that just sent packets of data – without caring what that data was, whether language, maths, images, voice, video or something else. Translating it and working out what to do with it would be up to the computers: the network could be agnostic, which meant you could connect different computers, with different operating systems, to one another – something previously impossible.

If you'd told the people working on ARPANET that forty to fifty years later its successor would be transmitting voice and video, the idea wouldn't shock them: it had, Crocker said, occurred to several of them at the time.

IN PRACTICE, OF course, the shiny promise of technology rarely lives up to the reality when you try to get everything to work. The universities had hired contractors to deliver the kit they would need to get networked. UCLA – Crocker's institution – took delivery of its router, the device that handles sending, routing and receiving data so the computer doesn't have to, around nine months after ordering it.

You may know routers better as the box you plug into your phone line or cable to connect to the internet, but in 1969 they were cutting-edge technology, and UCLA's took weeks to get set up after delivery. The second router was delivered to SRI, and set up shortly afterwards.

As Professor Kleinrock, Crocker's supervisor at UCLA and the overseeing academic for the ARPANET project, noted in his 2014 conversation – 'SRI ... 400 miles up north – connected their IMP [Interface Message Processor, now referred to as a router] to their host, so now we had two hosts. Now we had a network. One node a network does not make. Two nodes, it does.'

This takes us to the moment that opened the chapter. The network might now work for two computers, but how would it handle data when it was flowing across the four machines intended to be linked up? What if it got as big as, say, a dozen computers?

This is a key area where the funding having come from ARPA – in other words, from the US government's defence budget – helped shape what happened next, and thus helped shape the internet. The academics acting as the nominal directors of the project were happy to work with the government and to take its funding, but ultimately were concerned with pursuing their own academic interests, rather than simply taking orders from the government as researchers on the payroll might.

This meant ARPA wasn't strictly dictating the terms of the experimental network as it would for an in-house project. But, quite often, neither were the senior academics overseeing the project, who were themselves scattered across multiple institutions and corporations, and who often saw the network project as a sideshow.

That left our assortment of relatively young postgraduates having to make and agree design decisions – with no one in charge day-to-day. This had major consequences. One was that, given the network had been designed to be able to connect different types of computers and devices together, it was clear it could (and likely would) be extended from the four institutions it began with. This meant that no one tried to make a final decision, or a finished product. Instead, like a construction kit, they were building a foundation that could be built upon, or altered: an open network.

Another consequence came about essentially because of bids to avoid fights: if no one is in charge and everyone has different ideas, how do you document what you're doing and why, or set your standards? You certainly can't just proclaim a new rule without provoking a backlash. It was Steve Crocker who hit on a solution – the main reason for his inclusion in the Hall of Fame. And it's not a revolutionary piece of code. It's not code at all. It's a piece of office politics.

'We were just graduate students,' he said in his speech to the Internet Hall of Fame.[7] 'Nobody put us in charge. We had no authority. And it fell to me to organize these notes that we had decided that we were going to write, and I found myself extremely nervous that as I said the act of writing these notes might trigger a negative reaction.

'So I hit upon this silly trick of saying well, we'll just call every one of them, no matter what they are – They might be super formal or they might be completely informal. But we'll just call every one of them a "request for comment", as a matter of form. And I thought that this was a temporary device that would last a few months until the network was built and we had organized manuals and documentation and so forth.

'So here we are more than forty years later, Requests For Comments are still the lingua franca for the standards process.'

Crocker wrote the first Requests For Comment in April 1969 – and fifty years later, RFCs are still the governing system issuing the protocols by which the internet works. The process for issuing and agreeing them has become more complex – and the stakes much higher (as examined in The Custodians) – but there's still no one institution in charge.

FROM THIS FIRST connection came a nascent network, which grew slowly throughout the 1970s. This growth, though, was itself more driven by ARPA than is commonly remembered – researchers did not immediately hear about the interconnected computers of the ARPANET and want it. They worried, instead, that connecting could only spell out bad things for them. They already used their own computer 100 per cent of the time, after all, so what possible benefit could there be in letting other people join the queue, too?

This is where ARPA's status as a big potential funder gave it some power to shape what would come next, and also why the driving motive of ARPA for funding this kind of work begins to come clear. No one will ever be able to give one definitive motivation – even within the agency different people had different reasons for supporting the project, and have different recollections – but we can look at some of the most prominent.

Networking was struggling to take off within individual campuses – let alone across rival universities – because of bureaucratic infighting, budgetary fights and academic jealousy. Technological challenges barely got a look-in; very few people seemed to want any part of it. And then came DARPA (renamed ARPA in 1972), a major funder for many universities, on its tour seeing what projects people had, and what they might want funding for.

Here's how Kleinrock recalled the issue in 2014,[8] reporting on what PIs – primary investigators, a term for the lead academic on a project that has received a funding grant – said when DARPA suggested they network.

'DARPA came in and said to all of the PIs around the country, "Let's put you in a network so we don't have to give you all the resources. You want to use a resource, you want to use graphics? Log on to a machine at Utah. You want to use a database? Log on to a machine at SRI."

'Almost uniformly, every one of them said, "We want nothing to do with a network. How can I possibly take my mainframe, all my time-shared system, and put it on a network and you're going to steal cycles from me? It's loaded now 100 per cent of the time."

'And so they said no. DARPA said, "Well, we're funding you guys. You shall join this network."

'[The universities] caved in and they did. Almost immediately, they were thrilled that this thing was working.'

DARPA didn't just fund the early internet, they also had enough clout and government connection to shape who joined it in the early days when ARPANET access was tightly controlled. As this technology had been funded by the US government, the government and military bodies wanted to benefit from the technology. But given the sensitivity of the data they handled, they didn't want to share everything on the network entirely openly. What these early adopters needed from the network – often, a bit of distance and protection from it – proved hugely significant.

Essentially, because the US was keeping a close eye on the progress of ARPANET, other government agencies were starting to notice the potential of networking.

'Even within the US, even within the US government, you had different agencies saying "Oh, we have to have a network too",' Crocker recalls. 'You had the Energy Department who wanted to connect its research laboratories together. You had NASA wanting to connect its laboratories together, and then the other was the National Science Foundation, I think. Clearly, those networks would want to be interconnected.'

Those three organisations would eventually want networks of their own, so they could share data within their institutions – but would also want to be able to share some, but not all, of their access and their information across a broader network. Those still working on ARPANET realised these needs would only increase as other countries joined the network, and as there became more ways to share data: in an ideal world, you would be able to send data across the same network via phone lines, radio waves, satellite and so on.

This is what led to the logic which turned ARPANET into the internet: the idea that what was needed was a 'network of networks'. That's the theory that lies at the very heart of the internet today, and one that affects us daily, even if we barely notice it. The fact is hidden in plain sight: 'internet' is simply a portmanteau of 'inter-', meaning between or among, and 'net', a shortening of networks. As names go, it's more functional than creative.

We have our home network, with our laptop, phone and smart speaker all connected to our home router. We might have a similar network (often called an 'intranet') at work, letting us do our jobs. And we can often connect in to one from the other, accessing our work files from home for example, via the internet – the network of networks.

That idea is so ingrained to modern life that it seems obvious, the only way things could be – but it was the result of a string of deliberate decisions, forced compromises and practical solutions along the early days of ARPANET and the internet. The basis of how the internet works was set out – in Request For Comment 675[9] – in December 1974, by a team of developers led by Vint Cerf.

Traffic on the internet still flows based on the system, known as TCP/IP, set out in that document. The 'TCP', Transmission Control Protocol, governed how data could reliably be sent through this network of networks with minimal errors, allowing communications to be broken up into 'packets' of data which were then reassembled into coherent form at their destination – a crucial component of such a network.[10]

This 'packet' system works differently from the way phone calls worked at the time. For a phone call, a single section of cable would be used to connect the caller and the recipient, sometimes attached with the aid of a human operator. For the duration of the call, they would have sole use of a phone connection (for example, between an office in Boston and one in Atlanta), even if data was only being sent along it when they were speaking.

Under the packets system, whatever is being sent – voice, text, a download – is split into numerous equal-sized 'packets' of information, each one essentially in an envelope which says where it was sent from, where it's going, how many packets there are in total, and what number it is in that sequence.

Each packet can then take any route it wants between its source and destination, and arrive in any order – no single cable connection is exclusively tied up, no packet needs to know what route another is taking, and the network can be used much more efficiently. As a bonus, if any particular connection goes down, it's no big deal – the data can simply take another route. Once all the packets have arrived at the far end, they're juggled back into the right order and reassembled.

The other half of the system, 'IP' – Internet Protocol – took longer to formally coalesce, but essentially consisted of giving each computer (or sometimes, each network) a unique series of numbers at which it could be found. On the modern internet, each typed web address (like www.jamesrball.com) corresponds to a numerical IP address (in this case, the Squarespace server my website sites on, at 198.185.159.144, in a data centre not far from Wichita, Kansas) – and TCP still governs what gets sent and received if you type that in.

Part of the internet philosophy of being a lightweight network of networks – which just sends data around the planet and lets the computer worry about decoding it – means it's easily expandable, both geographically and politically.

This meant ARPANET could be expanded transatlantically early in its life: in 1973 the first message was sent from a UK university, University College London, to the previously US-centric network.[11] This was, in a small way, revolutionary in a world in which more distance had always meant more cost.

'There were no fees in the ARPANET,' Crocker notes. 'Generally, so you don't get charged for how far you send a packet. You don't get charged even for how many packets you send.'

It also meant the network could be expanded in what it was able to do, as new protocols were agreed. One of the first of these was email, developed in 1971. And new networks could be added with limited concern – because each network chose what to share with the wider global internet, no one had to worry too much about who was added.

That doesn't mean the growth of ARPANET was then simple, or without tension. The US Department of Defense had led the charge on networking, and the network that resulted, in order to function, was one that resisted central control.

'How much of the defense drive was pushing development of this ARPANET? It is a mixed story. It'll never be a complete story,' was Professor Kleinrock's conclusion in his public talk.

One man with a good idea of the answer was Steve Lukasik, who – as first deputy director, and then director of ARPA – was the man who signed the cheques for most of the early days of

ARPANET, and who in a later reflection described the project as a 'high-risk gamble' suitable to the agency's mandate, and one which definitely had 'unexpected results'.[12]

Unsurprisingly, according to Lukasik's account ARPA was not especially concerned with computer use at a handful of US universities. The problem the agency was grappling with was command and control – partly for the US military as a whole, but primarily for the country's Cold War nuclear arsenal.

Packet switching provided an opportunity for the nuclear deterrent: if its promise of splitting up signals so they could be sent dynamically across the country, or across the world, even if some pathways were disrupted or destroyed, was confirmed, that would have huge potential. Even if most of the connections were destroyed by an adversary, signals could still get through if some remained – exactly what you want from a weapons system of last resort. But the system would have to be reliable and proven, so why not fund academics to test it in a lower-risk environment?

That does not mean that the researchers and early pioneers were knowingly assisting the USA's nuclear efforts – at least not by Lukasik's account. 'The bulk of the ARPA contractors involved were unaware of, nor did they particularly care, why the DoD was supporting their research,' he observed.

DARPA's relationship with the network and the community it had created and funded became an uncomfortable one throughout the early days of the internet, during which period the network grew slowly. The USA added more military sites, but soon academic growth outstripped the military.

By 1975, DARPA handed official government oversight of the ARPANET over to the Defense Communications Agency, who attempted to prevent unauthorised access to the network, despite it having no built-in tools to track accesses or use. Eventually, the military aspects of the network – parts which later became the basis for modern secure networks for diplomatic and intelligence information – were split from ARPANET, which was then wound down as its successor, the internet we know now, supplanted it.

'ARPA's intent had been to demonstrate the utility of packet switching for military command and control, and in that it succeeded brilliantly,' Lukasik's paper ruefully notes. 'As a consequence unanticipated by its sponsor, the ARPANET and its successor, the Internet, further demonstrated the general utility of networking for "command and control" far beyond the needs of the DoD.'

Overall, Lukasik seems unsure about the long-term results of the project he funded. By his account, he was focused on the short-term and foreseeable issues, and left the long-term to fix itself – and then when the specification found itself in the hands of ambitious grad students, it turned into something else.

'We did not attempt to follow all possible moves ahead and plan how we would prevent unexpected and undesirable consequences,' he concludes. 'To attempt to do so before proceeding would have paralyzed us to inaction, assuring that nothing positive would be accomplished. On balance ARPA and its developers protected the nation from one kind of technological surprise, only to create another.'

The internet, then, grew out of a muddled collaboration between three factions. The first was a defence research agency looking for a testing ground for future command-and-control programmes, who then saw potential in using the network for military research and development. The second group was headed by senior academics in leading research universities, most of whom wanted to use the funding and the network for other research opportunities – with people like Professor Kleinrock, whose research interest *was* networking, serving as the exemptions. And the third was the graduate students left to actually build the thing, whose superiors thought they were doing gruntwork, and who were in fact going well beyond their brief in the most interesting of ways.

No wonder no one got what they expected.

It's also perhaps no surprise, given the ambiguity of the internet's origin story, that there are several confused versions of it in circulation – ironically enough, mostly posted online.

One that has caught on, and which makes sense once you know the confusing truth, is that the internet was conceived as part of a bid to create a communications network that could survive a nuclear war. While that doesn't seem to have been the case, it's clear where the confusion could have come from.

It is, however, a story Steve Crocker – one of very few people to have seen ARPANET as both a university researcher and an ARPA staffer, working under Lukasik – finds easy to dismiss: he once talked the US military into taking the whole network out by accident. It couldn't survive his bright idea, let alone a nuclear strike.

Shortly after joining DARPA, he visited an air-force base and gave them advice on testing how much throughput the network had: they could try sending one message through lots of links at a time, 'like a Gatling gun'. Nerdy chat over, he left and thought nothing more of it.

Months later, the air-force technicians he'd advised tried out his system – and immediately overloaded every single router on the ARPANET, taking the entire system down, with no fallbacks, no automatic restarts, nothing. After the network was laboriously and manually rebooted, the confused technicians tried it again, wondering what had gone wrong. The whole network fell down yet again.

There were quite a few arguments in the fallout of the incident, Crocker recounts. But no one was fired.

'If this had been a deliberate project to build a nuclear-hardened thing and there had been a flaw in it that permitted a casual error like that to bring it down, I believe heads would have rolled. That would be totally unacceptable in a hard-core military oriented network. In a research network, different matter.'[13]

The internet – or ARPANET – hadn't been intended as some last-ditch communications network for post-nuclear-war life. It was built as a test bed, and then, seemingly without anyone's intent, it evolved.

THE MILITARY FUNDING and the confused multiple purposes of the internet meant its early growth was restricted to major institutions – at least at first. In October 1969, ARPANET had two nodes (a term for each router connected to a network), one in UCLA, and the other at SRI, 400 miles to the north.

By January 1970, all four of the initial nodes had been hooked up to the network. By the end of that year, another nine institutions had been connected. There then followed a wave of US military and government R&D sites, accompanied by a slower wave of academic institutions. But it would be an ambitious gambler at the end of the 1970s who said this would become an inescapable global network – even late in the 1970s, there were fewer than a hundred institutions connected.

The internet gradually expanded over two decades: almost everyone on the network knew everyone else. If there was a problem, they could phone each other; they met up at conferences, they were all from the same expert technical communities. Protocols were developed and tested slowly, often taking years from proposal to adoption.

Logging and security were largely afterthoughts – this was, after all, a trusted network. Very little was monitored, very little checked for tampering. Fundamentally, this has meant security has had to be tacked on to the internet a piece at a time, at scale, as it has become increasingly important to the world: there was no chance to build it in from the get-go, because it wasn't a worry at the time.

Otherwise, though, the slow growth meant that many of the key standards of the internet were solid and scaleable even when the online community was tiny. The separation of the US government's formal military network from ARPANET in the early 1980s increased the scope for expansion, as did the formal adoption of TCP/IP and other public standards. The internet grew steadily through the 1980s, but a new innovation at the end of that decade set the ground for much more.

This is the bit of the internet's story that is familiar to many of us: that of the British technologist Tim Berners-Lee, then a scientist at the European CERN institute, who came up with a document, submitted to his supervisor on 12 March 1989: 'Information Management: A Proposal'.[14]

The proposal, which was marked by Berners-Lee's supervisor as 'vague, but exciting', did not immediately set the world on fire, but in practice united many of the elements of 'the mother of all demos' with the architecture of the internet. The paper became the basis for what we now know as the World Wide Web – the internet as seen through your web browser – with its web addresses (formally known as URLs or URIs), HTML (the language used to format and style web pages) and HTTP (the protocol used to receive information on the web).

In practical terms, Tim Berners-Lee's discoveries set the ground for the internet to become a consumer product, and they did it just as the network was ready to consider connecting the networks and services of commercial entities to the internet's architecture.

The consumer internet effectively began here – but it was never going to become like the highly controlled telephone networks (of which more next chapter), because the culture had two decades to establish itself.

'A huge turning point was when it was determined that it was okay to have commercial versions of the internet, and they'd be interconnected,' Crocker explains. 'Now you had this huge explosion around 1990, 1991, and so forth, and then you take off ... Those traditions were set and that permitted anybody to innovate and let market forces determine whether or not those things would succeed or not succeed. That was quite different from the traditions and history of the telephone system in which the standards were set in stone and control very tightly and everybody had to implement things.'

The acceleration of the internet's growth, even seen in hindsight, is first glacially slow and then too fast to see. In 1970, the internet had around ten hosts (a term which at least in the earlier days of the internet roughly meant a connected computer). By 1977, it had around a hundred. It took until 1985 – another eight years – to get to a thousand. It crossed 10,000 by 1987, sat around 100,000 by 1990, and then crossed one million before 1993.[15]

Today, around half the world's population are connected to the internet[16] – and the total number of devices connected to it is estimated at around 25–30 billion, or four for each person on the planet.[17]

Crocker, someone who could be said to have had an integral role building this system that's now fundamental to the modern world, talks about the network he helped create with an odd disconnect. On the one side is the small experimental project he worked on early in his career. On the other is a global network of billions – the two simply don't feel like the same thing.

Crocker had quickly moved on from ARPANET, which he had seen as a distraction from his main research interest – only to get drawn back into the protocols and governance of the internet years later. On one level, he says, the way the internet was built was ready for something as big as it has got: it was designed to let different machines connect, to scale, to work without central command and control. On another, what kind of person would expect not only to have a role in creating something like the internet, but also to live long enough to see it go from revolutionary to so ubiquitous that it's virtually invisible? On the practical matters, Crocker finds it easy to spot what they missed – everything connected to the internet needs an IP address, for example.

Once it seemed like a few dozen addresses would be plenty. Then they realised they were going to hit that limit. So they re-engineered it to a limit so high they knew they'd never hit it – around four billion. And then, some years later, it became clear four billion would soon not be enough – and they had to rebuild the architecture once again, but this time of a sprawling global network unlike any other.

'On the ARPANET, the addressing structure was a relatively small number ... up to about sixty,' he recounts. 'By the time I'd turned my attention elsewhere, the decision was made to have thirty-two-bit addresses. Thirty-two-bits gives you, if you use all of them, four billion. If I thought sixty was large ... four billion is bigger than sixty. Then you get to this awkward point where that turns out not to be big enough.'

Crocker set out various technical considerations where they had made it difficult to re-engineer addressing and other structures, and says from a design perspective he regretted it now that people were having to re-engineer it on a grand scale. But a bigger problem – more philosophical than practical – is security.

Noting that encryption technology was still in its infancy – and being closely guarded as a state secret at the time – and that it would have slowed down the development of the network even if they'd had it, he nonetheless notes the growing pains for an inter-university connection becoming the global communications backbone.

'In those days users were around time-sharing systems and each time-sharing system had a management structure,' he explains. 'If somebody was misbehaving, you'd call up the appropriate authority and say, you've got a guy there who is screwing up. Somebody would tap them on the shoulder and say, "Stop doing that!" That doesn't work when you've got billions of users around the world and total anonymity and so forth. That's a bit more problematic.'

As to what the internet has done to the world, and how and whether it's changed power, concentrated power, challenged power, or done something else, Crocker is philosophical. Ever the engineer, he prefers to ask questions rather than answer them, not settling on anything definitive.

'On the power question … I suspect we haven't even begun to scratch the surface,' he muses. 'What is this going to do for governments? How is government power going to evolve? How is the power of banks and other financial institutions going to evolve … ?'

Eventually, he hits on a conclusion – of sorts.

'You get this rather utopian view that it distributes power … I think the more realistic thing is that you get different distributions of power. It's not a continuation of the old order and it's not the utopian thing, it's something different. Well, that's a lot harder to deal with because it doesn't have a simple predictable model. If you knew precisely what was going to happen, you could become very rich or very powerful … or both.'

When Crocker first experienced it, the internet was a single connection of a few hundred miles between two academic institutions on the West Coast of the USA. Today its backbone is a network of more than 1.2 million kilometres of cabling tying together every continent on the planet via billions of machines.[18]

It must, I say, be quite something to have been in the room to see the very first two-letter message – 'LO', then a computer crash – to set out how the growing network made its rules, and then see it encompass the world, fifty years on.

'I've been reflecting on it,' he says. 'It's an almost out-of-body experience of that happening. I was there, but it feels like I was an observer as opposed to … A lot of it happened, I did some small pieces of it. I was part of it, but I don't feel a sense of ownership, or this was me exactly, because there were a lot of people involved. It is interesting and it's been a hell of a ride, yes. You live through these transformations and you look back and you see how much has changed. It's been cool.'

2

The Cable Guys

MONA SHAW, A seventy-five-year-old retired air-force nurse living in Manassas, Virginia, had had enough. It was August 2007, and she had been kept waiting for her Comcast cable installation one time too many.

First, she told the *Washington Post*,[1] they had missed an appointment to install her new cable. Then they'd come two days late and got it half done. Then they managed to cut off the mediocre service they'd given her, and she and her husband went to the company's local office to complain. After leaving the elderly couple sitting in the blazing Virginia summer sun for two hours, the staff finally told them that the manager had left and no one would see them.

So two days later, Mona Shaw returned – with a claw hammer.

Shaw, described by the newspaper as 'a nice lady who lives in a nice house', who volunteered with her local square-dancing club and took in seven stray dogs from her local shelter, smashed a Comcast rep's phone, keyboard, monitor and more in a blaze of fury.

By the time the red mist had faded, local police and ambulance services were in attendance at the office, and Shaw was facing a three-month suspended jail sentence, a fine of \$345 and – unsurprisingly – a year-long restraining order keeping her away from Comcast's offices.

She also became briefly famous across America; but the problem for Comcast, beyond their smashed-up IT equipment, was that she was, if anything, a national hero for a country beyond sick of their cable company. It was safe to say Comcast, and the industry as a whole, had something of an image problem.

This was just one of many incidents that marked the sheer unpopularity of the USA's cable providers in the last years of the 2000s. The response – of Comcast at least – was to hire Frank Eliason,[2] the man who became, for a time, the face of one of America's most-hated industries.

Broadband gripes were hardly an issue restricted to the USA. In the UK today around one in six broadband customers are unhappy with their service – a worse proportion than many similar industries – and regulators receive thousands of complaints every year.[3] But it was Comcast that had become the symbol and the epicentre of a global, industry-wide problem.

'One of the things when I first started at Comcast, and it's going to sound strange … it was actually a good thing. I was sitting in my office and a regional vice president who was well over my level came to my office and said, "A year ago we would have never hired you," ' Eliason recalls. 'He didn't quite say it like that. He said it a little bit edgier. For at least a year I thought he was much taller than I was. For a year I didn't realise he was about a foot shorter than me.'

Eliason was a rare outsider in an industry known for only hiring its own – he had been brought in as a mid-level manager overseeing customer support, charged with trying to improve the image of an industry everyone hated. 'I was definitely not your typical cable employee,' Eliason notes.

Eliason is what you'd expect from a man who became the face of good customer service: optimistic, charismatic and scrupulously keen to listen and understand your concerns. His rise to fame came thanks to the internet his company and its rivals supplied to American households: having seen customers complain about Comcast across Twitter, he – of his own volition – set up the @ComcastCares Twitter handle, and began single-handedly interacting with hundreds, then thousands of customers directly.

Twitter customer service might be business-as-usual today, but in the mid-2000s this was a ground-breaking initiative and led to Eliason being profiled in business and technology magazines time and again – becoming arguably more famous even than the company's CEO (then and now), Brian Roberts, the son of the company's founder and the man who turned a middle-of-the-road cable company into one of the USA's most powerful corporations.

Frank Eliason found himself the face of the cable industry, and what it was doing to its public – whether they were annoyed about losing their favourite channel from their cable TV package, or their internet wasn't working. He was used to dealing with angry customers. The hard part was that they so often had good reasons to be angry.

When we think of the internet, the money that's made there and the power relationships at its core, we rarely think of whatever company – whether via cable, phone lines, satellite or cell network – provides our actual connection to the internet. This is, perhaps, by design. Except for when we move house and we need to search for whoever might be able to connect us to the internet, it often feels as if these utility players prefer to be invisible, provided we keep paying our bills.

Internet service providers (ISPs) like Comcast in the USA or BT in the UK lack the glamour of the technology giants, but they don't lack revenues or profits. Because they take money directly from customers each month, rather than extracting it via advertising, they take more money, even if they have far fewer users than the social giants. Comcast operates almost exclusively in the USA, and yet took around $30 billion more than Facebook in revenue in 2018. For the average US internet customer that year, Comcast received $646.80 — more than $50 per month, for a simple internet hook-up.[4]

Unlike cable TV — packages of dozens or hundreds of channels, each of which can be sold separately, many at premium prices — the internet comes with very few overheads: you don't have to buy in channels or commission original programming. Despite networks' fears, ISPs can rake money in by being a 'dumb pipe' — just selling the connection, and not worrying about what data is flowing along the connection.

But where there are big profits, there is power — and the cable companies have plenty of that, too. They enjoy long-standing relationships with lawmakers, but they also have huge access to their customers' data. We might be more used to worrying what Google, Facebook or some advertiser holds about us, but your internet provider has a chance to access everything coming and going from your computer or phone, unless it's encrypted. This is another chance for power, money or leverage.

When you're the company responsible for actually shifting data from city to city, or continent to continent, your interests aren't the same as the companies making the content. It might suit Netflix to make video content HD, then super-HD, then ultra-HD — but each time they up the pixel count, that's more work and more cost for the ISP.

This type of battle — Silicon Valley versus ISPs — is a running one across the modern internet, and one which drags in users, activists, governments, regulators and the courts. Some ISPs had a simpler role in this fight, as they only had internet-era businesses, but others — like BT and Comcast — had their own conflicts of interest, working on old media like phones and pay TVs as well as the new era.

Since the cable companies and their fellow ISPs will play a big role in the battles depicted throughout this book, we need to know what makes them tick. Thankfully, as Frank Eliason puts it, that's usually simple: the cable companies are refreshingly old-fashioned in their goals. They rarely claim to be changing the world. They're all about the bottom line.

'Truthfully, for the most part, the internet does not cost the cable companies much money in the overall scheme of things on a per-subscriber basis,' he says. 'You made fifty bucks a month, it'll probably cost them like five. It's a hugely profitable set-up.'

Keeping those kinds of profit margins doesn't happen by itself: if there are enough other companies who could provide a customer's internet, someone will eventually undercut you, selling that $5-a-month service for $45, instead of $50. Maintaining your market position relies on dissuading would-be competitors from sinking in the huge upfront costs involved in the business, keeping the rules on your side, and more.

But that's not the only move the cable giants have to be aware of: they also have lost ground to make up for, as the internet lures a generation of would-be cable TV buyers away from the expensive multi-channel packages they might otherwise have bought. The internet might be good money and good margin, but if your business elsewhere is ebbing away, and shareholders want their returns, you've got to go further.

The result? More potential for conflict between the people who provide the internet connections and the ones who provide its content.

As Eliason explains, that means a conflict of interest for the cable companies, now facing the much lower-profit proposition of supplying internet to homes, and then watching other firms get revenue providing services that replace the premium television they'd prefer to offer.

'Their model is now pure internet,' he says.

The dream, if you're a cable company, is to be able to profit from both sides of the connection: to charge the customer for giving them access to the internet, and then to charge websites for delivering their content to customers. That's not always possible, but the principle of cable companies offering some websites faster, or priority, access to their users has been a tempting one – and a prospect fiercely fought off by the internet giants.

This battle is known as the net neutrality debate – based on the idea that all traffic on the internet, all packets of data (whether voice, text, image or video) are treated in the same way, no matter who sent them or where they're going. For some, it's high principle, while others see it as a standard tussle between large corporations. Either way, there is big money at play.

That's just one of the reasons the cable companies have to interfere in the workings of the internet. Another is found in their own internal conflicts of interest – as Comcast perhaps demonstrates better than anyone. Comcast doesn't just run networks of cables: it's a huge producer of content, as owner of both NBC, one of the USA's major networks, and its movie division, Universal Studios.

If you make content, you're likely to worry about internet piracy, and when industry fears about piracy were at their peak in the late 2000s, Comcast went a step too far in its efforts to stop it – and got caught.

Robb Topolski, a former Intel engineer – and a Comcast customer – had set up his computer to share his music folder with peer-to-peer file-sharing services, but got curious when no one appeared to be trying to share his music. After some detective work, later picked up by reporters at the Associated Press, he deduced that Comcast was stopping the file-sharing service working – not by openly blocking the traffic, but instead using deceptive means to effectively break the software.[5]

If your company is responsible for providing access to the internet – a service increasingly becoming people's primary source of news and information – and you've been found to be secretly tampering with it in your own corporate interests, you will face a well-deserved backlash.

That's just a small part of the battle, the bit visible to consumers, and Comcast's conduct in this arena made explaining other headaches to its customers far more difficult. That was another problem that would land on Frank Eliason's desk: so far as most customers are concerned, Comcast provides their internet. If a website doesn't work, or if something is blocked, or there is some other issue, well ... it must be Comcast's fault, right?

The accusation from the customer, Eliason says, becomes 'you're blocking me'. And that's a problem 'especially with a company like Comcast'. The headache for Eliason was that Comcast on occasion *had* blocked access for its customers to certain sites, meaning the customers often weren't sympathetic to the argument it wasn't Comcast's fault this time – even though that was often true.

What's usually going on, though, isn't blocking so much as errors. Tracing how these occur reveals a hidden layer of activity most of us would never think about, and the next commercial battleground of the online world.

When most of us pay our cable company (or phone company, or whoever) for our internet access, that's about the last we think of it. Some of us have 'unlimited' monthly deals that let us view, download or stream however much we want – within vague 'fair use' restraints – and not worry about it. Our monthly bill will be the same whatever we do. For other users, there is some monthly cap of data, a certain number of gigabytes as a limit, beyond which more data use will be charged.

What we don't worry about is getting charged more for visiting a website hosted in Sweden versus one in Ohio, or being billed by a different company if our Netflix video stream comes via Ireland rather than transiting through the UK. None of that stuff ever crosses our radar: whichever company we pay for access seems like the be-all and end-all of the internet.

That's not remotely what's going on behind the scenes. Ever since its inception – as seen in the last chapter – the internet has always been conceived of as a 'network of networks'. In the early days of ARPANET, this was very simple: each of the first four institutions had one computer, these were networked together, and ARPA paid the bills.

Eventually, some institutions had a few of their own computers, and didn't want to just hook everything up to ARPANET. So these ran their own networks, then in turn connected those to ARPANET – and once again, the US government covered the bills. And so it continued, with the network getting ever more complex and multilayered – but the US government stopped footing the bills years ago.

What hasn't changed is that every computer and every cable belongs to someone. The wireless or wired network inside your house – connecting your computer to your router – likely belongs to you. The cabling to your local area's telecoms box probably belongs to whoever you buy your internet from, as does a lot of the cabling in your city.

Since the early days of the internet as a consumer product available to homes – a revolution sparked mainly by Tim Berners-Lee's work on the far more accessible World Wide Web as a gateway to the internet – it has piggybacked on existing telephone networks. In the 1980s and 1990s the few people who used internet services at home would do so via dial-up internet, in which a modem in their home would convert the digital signals back to old-fashioned analogue and send it over the phone lines – as anyone who accidentally picked up a handset would know, it sounded like a series of ear-splitting beeps.

Today, things have effectively flipped. As data becomes the main form of transmission, and phone networks themselves go digital, voice and phone signals are now sent along data cables, which have widely been upgraded from copper to fibre-optic, in all but the last few metres to most people's homes. In towns and cities, it's still those telecoms companies who generally own and operate the cabling.

Eventually, though, it will interface with a cable that belongs to someone else – if your connection needs to go from the UK to the USA, it needs to go across one of the transatlantic fibre-optic cables, all of which also have an owner.

The most obvious thing this means for most of us is that when something goes wrong, it might not actually be your internet provider's fault: any connection to any website is likely to travel across multiple different networks and computers, owned and managed by totally different people or corporations.

The easiest way to see what this means in practice is to actually look at it. Any computer can look up what route it's currently taking to access any website, or any particular online address, using a tool called 'traceroute'. The text below is the real output when my computer in north London tries to connect to Twitter:[6]

1 bthub (192.168.1.254) 2.182 ms 3.725 ms 2.480 ms

2 * * *

3 * * *

4 31.55.186.188 (31.55.186.188) 22.822 ms 23.552 ms 24.048 ms

5 195.99.127.94 (195.99.127.94) 23.502 ms
core3-hu0-6-0-3.faraday.ukcore.bt.net (195.99.127.194) 22.314 ms
host213-121-192-120.ukcore.bt.net (213.121.192.120) 22.590 ms

6 peer6-hu0-12-0-0.telehouse.ukcore.bt.net (213.121.193. 189) 23.932 ms
213.121.193.191 (213.121.193.191) 24.328 ms

peer6-huo-12-0-0.telehouse.ukcore.bt.net
(213.121.193.189) 24.062 ms
7 xe-1-1-0.cr1-lon1.twttr.com (195.66.225.142) 23.625
ms 25.017 ms 25.550 ms
8 104.244.42.129 (104.244.42.129) 23.949 ms 29.694 ms
23.778 ms

To most regular humans, the above looks like complete gibberish – because frankly, it is – but it's gibberish that can be decoded. Each number is a hop in a chain of connections between my computer and Twitter, the website it was aiming to reach.

Here's roughly what the text above tells you: my computer first gets in touch with the router in my London flat, 'bthub' – which lets you know my internet provider is BT, or British Telecom. After a bit of delay (that's the '* * *' in 2 and 3), it ends up bouncing around a few nodes within BT's network in London – the stops we see with the long numbers beginning '195'.[7]

It is possible to turn an IP address into an approximate real-world location – it's as simple as typing the sequence into one of many free online geolocation services, such as iplocation.net. If we do this we can see where the request travels.

At 6, the signal jumps again to another spot within BT's network, which appropriately given its former status as the national telecoms provider is the most comprehensive in the UK. These machines are located in Wales – but the signal soon bounces back to London at point 7, and leaves BT's network, going to a server in Twitter's name ('lon1.twtter.com') in London. From there, it makes its final stop – to a server in a Twitter data centre in Kansas, from where I can get the website I would like to see.

This connection is pretty simple – most of the stops along the way actually belong to the company I pay for my internet. But Twitter doesn't actually own any of the undersea cables across the Atlantic, so is paying someone for its use, meaning that this route shows at least some money must change hands.

That's not an unreasonable proposition, as building and maintaining the transatlantic cables is something of an astonishing task. The cables are smaller than you might think – about the width of a hosepipe for much of their distance, and most of that is just armour for the tiny fibre-optic core – but need to be laid, maintained and monitored.

When they get to shallow water and the shore, they are typically buried, partly to avoid damage and partly to somewhat obfuscate their route to prevent sabotage – but at sea they can be damaged by tides, heavy trawling nets, and even on occasion by shark attacks.[8] Repairing a cable deep in the ocean is no trivial task – boats have to find both broken ends of the cable, bring them on deck and replace the destroyed section.

Each of our internet tasks requires our request to flow across cable systems owned by multiple people, through data centres, routers and other machines owned by more people, and we expect all of these transactions to happen in the course of simple microseconds.

This is the level of activity happening just beneath the surface every time we do anything on the internet, and it's this that every single internet provider has to pay attention to and take note of.

They might choose to share access to their own networks with other providers if they think it will all work out fairly evenly, but if you're a company that owns large parts of the international backbone of the internet – known as a 'tier one' provider – you are going to want to charge money to all the national and local internet providers for making use of the asset you own.

The internet might have been created without thinking of billing, and many of the conventions that grew up in that era still exist – we still don't expect to pay any more or any less for data that's travelled halfway down our street than we do for data that's travelled twice around the world.

In general, the cost of sending data is cheap enough that data centres are located where electricity and land is cheap and plentiful but skilled workers are available. It's sometimes worth paying for the extra distance, and even new cabling, to get this. These decisions are invisible to us as users, but for the corporations that now make the internet work, trading in the right to send and receive our data is the hidden battlefield, with the winner taking the profits.

There is a lot more to the complex way our traffic flows across the globe. The routes it takes, and who can see it along the way, can shape what we see, if we pay to see it, who knows we've seen it and more.

One quick way to get a sense of what's happening is to send a 'ping' to a website. A ping is a very simple request to a website, essentially just saying 'hello' to a site and seeing how long it takes to get a response. This is used practically when diagnosing problems – it's a test of whether the computer is operating and on the network for the most basic of tasks, but we can also use it just to see what happens.

Here's what happen if I ping Stanford – home to one of the first two ARPANET connections – from the UK:

```
jamesball$ ping stanford.edu
PING stanford.edu (171.67.215.200): 56 data bytes
64 bytes from 171.67.215.200: icmp_seq=1 ttl=239
time=182.686 ms
```

What this mainly shows us is that my request got all the way to Stanford and back from the UK in 182.686 milliseconds – not bad, but not good enough for lots of the biggest providers. If

I try to ping Google – also based on the West Coast – I get a response in just 17 milliseconds, not because they have a faster cable, but because they replicate their data centres across the world to cut even more milliseconds from their search times, handily also reducing the need for data to flow transatlantically. In practice, this means Google has copies of the files, emails, search databases and more, in multiple huge out-of-town data sites around the world, reducing how often it has to send data across the oceans.

Traceroute gives us a window into an otherwise invisible world. But so far as customer service exec Frank Eliason was concerned, traceroute had a much simpler purpose: trying to prove to you that this time, for once, the reason you couldn't get to the website you wanted really wasn't Comcast's fault.

Now that managing the internet's complex and global network of networks is no longer the province of the single government agency paying the bills, it has turned into as much of a race for profit as anything else – and it's here perhaps that Comcast have got particularly creative.

Generally speaking there are two ways that internet providers can work with one another to use one another's cables. If you're a tier one company, managing cables which cross oceans and thus form the backbone of the global internet, you may find yourself often needing to use another tier one company's network to reach particular countries.

In these instances, provided traffic use is fairly even, such companies come to arrangements known as 'peering', where no money changes hands: the companies have set standards for who they'd be happy to work with on this basis, and who they'd consider it fair to give this kind of access.

If a company that only works to provide cabling in its local market, or even just in its own country, wants to use a tier one network, well, it doesn't have much to offer in return by comparison – so it's going to have to pay. This is known as paying 'transit', and is a fact of life for all but the biggest cable operators – you do what you can in your own network and with your peers, and then buy transit when you need it.

Under Brian Roberts, Comcast – which is not a tier one provider – found a different trick, as the company's then vice president Barry Tishgart set out at length to the online tech publication *Ars Technica* in 2014, amid controversy over its tactics.[9]

The company had aggressively expanded by buying up cable companies across the USA, which had traditionally operated as local and regional players – companies initially welcomed as agile competitors to the previous monopoly telecoms company, AT&T.

This increasingly meant Comcast had more and more customers on its networks – and, as it became a bigger deal, on the internet. Sheer number of customers is one thing, but Comcast's physical network became still another: it soon had the most comprehensive cross-USA cable network, and in that country only AT&T had a more comprehensive network full stop.

The USA is such a big market, and such an important and busy one, that Comcast essentially managed to persuade tier one internet providers – the real global cable giants behind the scenes – that they needed Comcast's network as much as it needed theirs. That meant it secured peering agreements, without any of the inconvenience and expense of laying or buying international cables.

The very existence of peering agreements hints at an era of share and share alike, of a 'fair play' internet, but Comcast's use of its US leverage to get access to such agreements revealed that era, if it had ever existed, was over: now that the internet is such a source of revenue and profit, whether in the content industry, retail cable or infrastructure, people will seek more revenues everywhere they can.

At this point, we start to get a picture of the commercial era of the internet – cable was the plucky upstart, fighting for the consumer against the telephone giants, and then they became the incumbents ready to be challenged.

Within a few years, we're told, 5G mobile phone service will be a reality, and early tests suggest it should be around ten times to fifteen times faster than 4G at its peak.[10] In practice, for many users, that means that the wireless internet could be as fast, or faster, than the wired internet we know now.

At its core the wireless internet is still the fibre-optic internet – but the so-called 'last mile' of cable or wire to your computer (or in practical terms, probably your phone) is replaced with 3G, 4G or 5G. The speeds of wireless will soon equal or surpass cable. It's not a fundamental change to the shape of the internet, but it's a chance for a whole new turf war for customers and standards between ISPs.

That would set off a whole new round of fights and of competition, as corporations vie to keep their share of our internet dollars. In theory, it would be easier to have multiple companies offering 5G in the same area than it would be to have multiple wired internet providers, increasing competition and initiating a squeeze against the cable companies and phone networks.

On paper, it seems that it would be good news for consumers – at least when the premium early adopter prices that will inevitably accompany the launch of a new internet technology begin to fall.

Whether or not it works out in our interests as consumers and as citizens doesn't, in the end, come down to finding which of the corporates has our best interests at heart – it comes down to ensuring lawmakers and regulators are looking out for us.

But the cable companies – and their rivals – are a step or two ahead of us here, too.

The cable companies are middlemen – in both a figurative and a literal sense. When it comes to the internet, most of us don't care too much who provides our connection, provided it's reliable and stays out of the way. We never get to see the wire, or the radio wave, that transmits our data to and from its intended destinations, so few of us feel strong affection for whoever provides it.

Perhaps partly as a result of this, the US cable industry – like many similar industries across the world – has never felt a particular need to be loved by the American public, as Frank Eliason realised after a couple of years of being with Comcast. He departed, back into the financial sector, in 2010 – two years into the global financial crisis, when banks were hardly at the peak of their popularity. Being the face of cable had taken its toll.

'It was actually extremely tough,' he explains. 'It's probably the reason I left. I really didn't think that they were changing fast enough and well enough – I told them this, so it isn't hiding anything ... The fact is we'd be selling my reputation. I've always, in any place I've worked, fought for the customer. That's what I do. It just didn't feel right.'[11]

Part of the reason for Eliason's discomfort, it seems, was the cable companies' savviness about who they really needed to keep happy to keep the profits rolling in – not so much their customers as the people who make the laws and appoint the watchdogs.

Research by the Federal Communications Commission found that more than 129 million US citizens – more than a third of the country's population – had only one company to 'choose' from when it came to receiving broadband. Why work hard to win the loyalty or business of a customer you literally can't lose?[12]

Profit then, instead, comes from keeping hold of that monopoly position for as long as you can, with favourable planning rules and other restrictions at the local level. At the national and international level, when your business model relies on numerous intricate negotiations with the Silicon Valley giants and other internet providers, anything lawmakers can do to tip the decks in your favour is also welcome.

The cable industry has had decades to hone this approach. Like most US industries, the cable sector isn't shy of spending on lobbyists in Washington DC – according to the OpenSecrets database, telecoms spent a total of $92 million lobbying Congress[13] (Comcast was first, with a $15 million spend) versus a $77 million Silicon Valley spend (just under $22 million of which came from Google's parent company, Alphabet).[14]

Like other major companies, cable corporates and their political action committees donate to candidates of both parties. But that's just the basics – the cable companies are much cleverer than that, when it comes to keeping the politicians onside.

'It's not about keeping the customer happy, it's about keeping the politicians happy,' Eliason alleges. This wouldn't just mean holding a nice drinks party, either. 'If you were a politician, you would actually get special servicing.'

In other words, if you were a politician, your cable company would make a note of it and ensure that you at least – if not necessarily the rest of your constituents – would get a great cable service, so you wouldn't think ill of your provider.

The rest of the time, the companies work as much as they can to adapt where there's competition, without making too much fanfare about it – so if you're lucky enough to have a choice of two or three cable companies to choose from, you'll get a much better deal from the same company than if you're in an area without that choice.

Eliason says it was possible to compare the service even from the same company – such as Comcast – in areas with competitors and without. So New England, for example, gets a lot more data per month than others.

'In our area, we don't have caps like in the rest of the country, where they have terabyte caps or something. It really comes down to if there's competition.'

In other words, unless they're forced to by competition or by government, the cable companies will get away with whatever they can.

If the people who actually provided the internet to our homes never got to be part of the utopian phase of the internet – when every Silicon Valley firm was heralded as a force changing the world for the better, and each CEO was a genius – it seems to have largely escaped any backlash.

Perhaps it's precisely because of missing the upside, and the intrinsic unsexiness of selling people access to a fibre-optic uplink. When a company is taking $50 a month from your account, ticking you off if you forget to pay it, and when it's also the first to blame when your internet fails exactly when you need it, it's hard not to see it as just another company.

Eliason, watching from his current vantage point as an independent consultant, sees this expectations game as part of the problem: our mistake, in his view, was to think of the internet companies as being any different from the cable ones.

'We had altruistic views of companies like Facebook,' he muses. 'They're trying to connect us to the world. They're trying to connect us to our friends. Whereas the cable companies are just trying to get us. Now, we're hitting a point where there's a realisation that even the Facebooks of the world are out to get us. They're out to get profit. Even though it's free, we're the product. They're not there to protect our privacy or connect to us, they're there to make money. It's actually going to probably be a little harder for those companies because they were so trusted for so long. Whereas, for the most part ... we never really trusted the cable company.'

The same is true – for Eliason at least – about the people who make the decisions which shape their respective companies. We talk about the CEO/founders of the tech giants as if they have unprecedented power over their businesses. And it's true that Mark Zuckerberg has created a structure that gives him control of Facebook's voting shares[15] – but Comcast, founded by its current CEO's father, has it written into its articles of incorporation that Brian Roberts shall be chair and CEO for so long as he lives and wants the job.[16] There is, it seems, nothing new under the son.

As Eliason sees it, a CEO is a CEO – he will think of himself as a pretty good guy, but his motivations aren't the same as yours. And in that respect, Zuckerberg and Roberts are very similar, despite often being on the opposite side of various conflicts.

'Ultimately, they're all proud people and they want to be the biggest. They want to be the best. That's oftentimes what lends itself to a lot of the issues that the cable companies have. It's the same issue … What they think is good and what their consumers think is good are two different things. What they think they're good at is being able to hire a lot of people, building a big company, et cetera. What their consumer thinks is being good is doing what's right by them. So it becomes a tug of war.

'Zuckerberg … is proud of his company. Just like Brian Roberts is proud of his company. But there is a thing in human nature where you want to be the best. The way we measure that is through the stock price, through your revenue, through these other means and it causes the problem.'

Facebook is a much younger company than Comcast – but in many ways it is far more consumer-facing, and more reliant on customer goodwill. More than 100 million Americans have no choice if they want a broadband internet connection. That's not true of anyone in the USA for Facebook – other social networks are available, even if some of them are owned by Facebook too. Or, of course, people can opt out of social networks entirely.

That gives Comcast scope to act against its customers' interests – or work with government to gain advantage that way – using methods that Facebook doesn't, or at least that we don't know about yet. Nowhere has this been more sustained (or more stunningly exposed) than when it came to working with Western governments to monitor their own citizens, their own customers and people across the world – as will be shown at length in the next chapter.

The motive behind all of these activities is easily summed up by Frank Eliason – a lifelong corporate executive, and hardly an enemy or even a critic of US capitalism – in just a few short sentences.

'Let's face it. Everybody's been trying to own the internet in some way. Now, maybe not own it … I will say profit the most off it.'

3

The Custodians

IN FEBRUARY 2014, I served as a formal witness to a frankly bizarre ceremony, in a nondescript industrial estate in El Segundo, Los Angeles.[1]

Security experts had gathered from around the world, and been admitted through a string of elaborate and high-tech safeguards: they had peered into an iris scanner, entered a keypad code and swiped in through an entry card system. They had passed through a man trap – a space in which you have to wait for the door behind you to lock as the one ahead opens – and then entered what's known as an SCIF – a sensitive compartmented information facility, a special room engineered so that no communications signals can get in or out, used to handle sensitive intelligence by the US and UK militaries and intelligence agencies, among others.

This gathering had nothing to do with armies or spies, though – instead the grouping had gathered to participate in a 'ritual' designed to improve trust in the internet. The object of the ritual was to renew a security key – a very long and theoretically uncrackable sequence of letters and numbers – for a 'core zone' of part of the internet governing web addresses, and how '.com', '.net' and so on are tackled when people try to visit sites. The idea of all of the scrutiny and the security was to show no one could tamper with it, that no NSA or corporate back doors existed, and so people could trust the security key it would generate, which would be used across the internet for the following six months.

The ultimate aim of this exercise was to try to give regular internet users like you and me reason to have confidence in one of the most fundamental aspects of using the internet: that when I type in google.com into my browser, I can be sure that I will definitely be taken to the actual servers of Google – and not somewhere else.

For obvious reasons, it's fairly essential that people can have confidence that when they type in a web address they get taken to the correct place. One of the most common fraud attempts on the internet is to try to send an unwitting user to a website that looks like, for example, their online bank, by sending a convincing-looking email that directs the user to a website and web address which looks a lot like the real one.

How much more dangerous would that kind of attack be if someone could redirect some or all traffic going to the *real* web address of that bank to go to their servers instead? Such an attack wouldn't just put bank details at risk – imagine a country with a repressive government using it to track who tried to log in to an activist or opposition group, or a homophobic government using it to track down people who tried to log in to a gay hook-up app.

Scarily, these attacks are very possible. The internet's address book – known as the Domain Name System, or DNS – is based on trust, vulnerable to attack, and none of this is just theoretical: these attacks have been seen in the wild, and have been used.

The Los Angeles ceremony I witnessed in 2014 was part of an effort to build a new, more secure system to restore trust and security to one of the internet's most essential services, to one of the systems working in the background upon which everything else relies. It is part of a story of what happens when you try to rebuild and repair something built as an experimental research network – ARPANET – on the fly, as it becomes a global utility.

It's also frequently a story of failure: six years later, despite everyone's best efforts, the system is virtually no more secure than it was then – and experts fear there's little prospect of that changing.

THE ROLE OF DNS is to turn the kind of online addresses we're familiar with – wikipedia.org, google.com, etc., known as domain names – into specific IP addresses, the actual address system for the internet, which denotes specific networks or individual computers.

In the early days of the internet, when only a handful of computers were on the network, the list of which domain names corresponded to which IP addresses could just be kept as a text file on one computer, which the other machines on the network could check when they needed to – for example, if they were looking for where to send a particular signal, especially if it was to a computer that machine hadn't contacted before.

As the network expanded, someone would have to manually update the text file with the name of the new computer added to the network. So if a university's maths department got a computer and attached it to the network, they might want the address math.university.edu (so their staff could be emailed, etc.). They would tell the person whose job it was to keep the text file of web addresses up to speed, and they would get to it, hopefully within a day or two. Once the text file joined up that math.university.edu name to the IP address of the new computer, it would be up and running.

This is not an exaggeration: this is how it actually worked on the internet, right through into the mid-1980s – the file was called HOSTS.TXT.[2] Other computers on the network made a copy of that file at certain intervals, to make sure they were up to date. A system like this is clearly just about good enough for a few dozen machines, but the prospect of someone having to keep such a list up to date now that there are several billion online devices is not so much impractical as downright impossible.

That's why in 1987 an RFC – the passive-aggressive 'requests for comment' that make up the internet's protocols – was issued suggesting a new system, the DNS, which would replace this list with something that updated dynamically, rather than manually, and would be distributed, rather than sitting on just one machine.

The system has been refined a few times since 1987, but now essentially works by specialist servers playing something like a game of telephone, asking each other whether they have the information they need – a bit like someone in an office standing up and shouting 'Does anyone have the phone number for Gavin in IT?' Just as someone might respond 'I don't have it, but I've got the IT switchboard, if that's any good', requests go via a series of steps – a server might direct you to two or three others, before finding one that says it can tell you where the web address you've typed in your browser should take you.

To see how this works in practice, it helps to look at the components of a web address. Let's take one we should all be fairly familiar with: https://www.google.com. This address has four parts. The .com, which initially stood for 'commercial', is called the top-level domain, which says broadly what sort of website an organisation is, and where it's located. So not-for-profits would use .org (organisation), the US government uses .gov, US universities use .edu, and then countries have their own domains, such as .fr for France.

There are a small group of highly trusted central DNS directories that say where to go for each of these top-level domains – the core of the internet's naming system – and these then direct people down the line to look in one of thousands of other directories for individual sites within each top-level domain.

The main bit of the address is the domain, the 'google' component, which will be directed to a particular IP address from one of those directories. The 'www' part, known as a subdomain, will then be used by Google to decide where inside its network your request will go. For Google, 'www' before the word 'google' will take you to search, whereas 'mail' in the same place would take you to Google's email service, 'maps' would take you to Google Maps, and so on. The 'https' part simply tells the computers concerned what type of request you're making – web surfing, email, file sharing or something else.

That's how things work in principle – a chain of computers guiding each request to its intended recipient. The danger, of course, comes if someone along that chain shouts the wrong answer. There are precautions to make this difficult, mainly relying on the fact that if 999 computers are shouting one answer and only one something different, the system will trust the former. But sophisticated operators – for example, people acting on behalf of a nation state – can work to divert traffic so that it passes through a server they control on its way to its intended destination, letting them steal login details or monitor traffic.

In January 2019, the security firm FireEye reported exactly this kind of attack, operating across the globe at 'an almost unprecedented scale'. It has 'identified a wave of DNS hijacking that has affected dozens of domains belonging to government, telecommunications and internet infrastructure entities across the Middle East and North Africa, Europe and North America', the firm revealed.[3]

The attack, which FireEye attributed as likely to be connected to Iran in its origin, was used to harvest login credentials of 'telecoms and ISP providers, internet infrastructure providers, government and sensitive commercial entities' – all by hijacking the trust-based DNS upon which the internet relies.

This kind of hijacking could also, if an attacker was able to get access to some of the key servers at the 'root' of DNS, be used to temporarily take down large parts of the DNS system, making the internet largely unusable, either for users from a particular country or more widely.

Given the pivotal role DNS plays on the internet, and its role as an essential utility, you might imagine the system was tightly controlled and guarded – but as so often with the actual protocols governing how the internet works behind the scenes, that is not the case.

The short answer as to who runs DNS is a US-based organisation called ICANN, short for the Internet Corporation for Assigned Names and Numbers, which is responsible for that 'core' area of the internet's DNS infrastructure.

On the face of it, ICANN looks like a hugely powerful organisation: it has responsibility for the rules that govern DNS, it is the body responsible for deciding how web addresses work, and who is eligible for them – should we have an .xxx? how about a .catsstink? or .england? ICANN, in a sense, decides. And as well as deciding many of these rules – or not – they also administer a lot of the key hardware and databases.

It seems, then, that we might have found an organisation that really wields some of the behind-the-scenes power on the internet, one of the bodies that really runs the nuts and bolts upon which the multi-billion public-facing dollar businesses are built. It's certainly connected to many of the 'star' names of the early internet – the people who were there at the start and built its protocols.

Jon Postel, one of the UCLA postgrads who worked on ARPANET, was instrumental to its founding, prior to his premature death in 1998.[4] Vint Cerf, the 'father of the internet', served as its chair, before being replaced by Steve Crocker. In the small world of early internet-era hipsters, ICANN has attracted the big names.

Göran Marby, ICANN's current CEO, is very keen to disabuse me of the notion of an all-powerful ICANN as he welcomes me into his Los Angeles office. Despite the internet industry's more famous connection to the Bay Area and San Francisco, ICANN has stayed close to the internet's original UCLA home. Marby, a former networking executive and regulator in his native Sweden, took over the helm of ICANN in 2016.

On hearing he was taking a role at the top of one of the organisations governing the internet, a friend of Marby's bought him an emergency stop button for his desk — as his friend had heard an old saying that the internet has no 'off button' — to which he draws my attention as we chat.

With his country's trademark bluntness, he throws aside the idea that his role is in any way chief executive of the internet. ICANN, he argues, has virtually no power. It runs virtually nothing. Its role, instead, is to bring people together to agree how things will work, to get consensus, and to try to keep the internet working as it should.

That role, he adds, is very narrow: it's not for him to worry what you're using the internet to do, for good or ill — his role is just to keep the internet working and to keep people in agreement on the core protocols.

'When someone really pushes me on this one I say, "How can you accuse the road if someone uses that to rob a bank?" You try to fix the problem with robbing the bank, rather than trying to make holes for everybody on the road. That's why I think a lot of the discussion has gone wrong. Because we represent, and you can come up with every acronym there is for it, we actually do represent the road, the ability for people to move on this network. We are not what you use the internet to get access to.'

ICANN's role is restricted entirely to managing the top level of domain names — who can have and who manages .com, .net, .org and the hundreds of similar domains, who administers the core (the 'root') of the DNS system, and how the rules and protocols that govern the system function.

But it has to do all of this through consensus – it has no power to impose change. It began as an offshoot of the US Department of Commerce, which had taken over the internet oversight role from the Department of Defense.

ICANN had always worked relatively independently and transparently, but as the internet grew in power and importance, the USA's semi-official oversight role began to become more contentious, especially in Russia, China and their allies, leading for calls for the UN or some other body to be given a formal role overseeing some of the key protocols, such as DNS and allocation of addresses.

These calls only heightened after the extensive revelations from NSA whistleblower Edward Snowden in 2013 and 2014. These are covered more extensively in Chapter 6, but in short showed the US abusing its role overseeing the internet's protocols and security to give itself access to intelligence from foreign powers. These scandals fed into years of talks to remove the USA's formal role overseeing ICANN, which was finally agreed early in 2016, and actually done very late in that year, right at the end of Barack Obama's term in office.[5]

The result of trying to make the situation less political, of course, is that the system is very political: the US no longer has a formal role overseeing ICANN, but the UN doesn't either. Marby sees this as a victory: the US government was induced, as he tells it, to give up its formal role in running the internet, with little more than just persuasion.

'How did we do that? We have participants from 130 countries around the world with thousands of people including governments, who came up with a plan,' he says. 'From 130 countries or 135, I can't remember, people from all backgrounds, all different stakeholders, with all interventions and civil society against people who want to make money, and they all came together. How often has that happened in the world? You have anything from democratic countries with long democratic traditions to countries who don't like democracy. All of them came together and we came up with something that works.'

And now that the organisation is truly independent, it's obliged to work with everyone to gain consensus and to move very slowly to keep everyone onside. Because if someone else wants to try to build something to replace it, there's nothing stopping them. The group was once a US government agency, and got some funding as such, but now pays for itself by taking a portion of fees from people buying online addresses. So if something else got enough support, they could in theory take over.

'If someone comes around with a better methodology to connect people, because that's what we do, we're connecting people, we should step aside,' says Marby. 'We are not doing this for any other reason than to provide a service to the world.

'The problem I see is that many people who want to have another technology do it for another reason. They do it because they don't like the governance model of ICANN. Which is actually a fairly good inclusive open methodology for governing something like us. The whole ecosystem is built on transparency and accountability. There are, of course, companies, individuals and even countries sometimes who don't like that model, because they would like to control this,' he says, speaking circumspectly and not naming particular nations – but referring to countries that wish to limit who can post information to the internet or have their own web address. Control over domain names for Hong Kong, Tibet or Crimea, for example, would all be highly political issues.

'They think anyone shouldn't be able to get an IP address, not everybody should be able to have a domain name. They use the discussion about technology for a political reason.'

Unpicking the minutiae of how ICANN reaches its decisions, and how it works them out, runs across dozens of policy documents, subcommittees and more. Its processes are best described as slow and, in all honesty, boring. When trying to work across hundreds of countries with no ability to force decisions, you work steadily and you work carefully – setting out consensus for each decision, and simply staying off the contentious stuff.

When looking at its processes, it's easy to dismiss ICANN as a sideshow, or something for the nerds. That's why it's important to step back and remember what they're running – essentially an addressing system that the whole world can agree to work with – and why they're the ones in charge of it. And in short, that's largely because no one can agree on anyone else to run it.

Nation states and private companies might be willing to give up on the idea of controlling something like the Domain Name System themselves – but they don't want to hand it over to a rival nation, or to some entity that could grow too powerful.

By keeping it in the hands of an organisation respected for its technical ability, but which has almost no political clout (or agenda) of its own, the potential for control of one of the internet's key protocols and levers is neutralised. The price of doing so, though, is to make the core of the internet sluggish: it can move only by consensus of lots of different players with lots of different motivations.

Trying to fix the infrastructure of the internet, then, is a little like trying to repair the engine of a sophisticated rocket ship. While the rocket is firing. While the ship is in space. And while it has billions of people on board. Given the risks of getting it wrong, you might just be tempted to leave the whole thing untouched – but that, too, might blow up the ship.

The core problem as Marby sees it is that the internet now has hundreds of thousands of internet service providers, some government-run, some private companies, all with their own priorities, and changing anything significant in practice needs all of them on board.

'If you want to change anything, and we are actually thinking how you can change it because we think we should do that, how do you convince 250,000, 300,000 ISPs out there at the same time?' says Marby. Changing things on the internet is *hard*.

Who runs the internet? Or even its infrastructure? Marby has a short answer.

'No one.'

IT'S WHEN THINGS come to practicalities that the difficulties of ICANN's position – and the oddness of real-world comparisons – become clear. And this is what returns us to the security ceremony which opened this chapter.

ICANN is trying to improve the security of the internet by tightening up the game of telephone that is DNS by guaranteeing identity of at least the central servers at its core – essentially providing assurances that servers are owned by who they say they are, to reduce the risks of impostors, the most direct risk of attack.

Online security and identity is usually guaranteed by encryption, and so the high-security ceremony in El Segundo was part of efforts to create a certificate (or code) valid for a period of months which would then vouch for the handful of servers at the very core of the system.

The theory was that, in turn, each DNS server could then also certify its own recommendations and listings – essentially like going from a system in which any server can shout 'Hi! I can tell you where to go for google.com' to some servers saying 'Hi! I can tell you where to go for google.com, and here's a shiny and almost-impossible-to-fake medal proving that I'm trustworthy!'

To make sure that experts weren't just having to take the creation of the certificate on trust – or trust anyone not to introduce security vulnerabilities or similar – there were numerous and elaborate security and transparency measures. These began with the extensive physical security at the site, but then moved on to steps requiring the event to be live-streamed, to have witnesses from multiple countries, and to require keys from multiple experts across the world.

This part of the system really appeals to fantasy nerds, working by having seven experts across the world, each of whom had a key for the West Coast certification ceremony – and each renewal would need at least three of the keyholders to be present in person, with their key. Once they have accessed and unlocked their keys from a safe in a room isolated from electronic signals, the certificate could finally be made.

Another seven experts had seven more keys for an identical ceremony on the East Coast, alternating with the West Coast one, to spread out responsibility for keeping the certificate valid. Finally, still another group of experts each held emergency backup keys, which could be combined in case of emergency to restart the whole system from scratch, should it ever be taken down or compromised. You couldn't accuse them of making it under-complicated.

In practice, the key cards work to approve a device that generates a new key code – in essence creating a system where seven people are authorised to approve the process, and at least three are required to do so. As soon as three key cards are in the machine, it will work and generate a new code. This is an over-simplification, but gives the general idea of the process.

This more secure system, if it caught on, would undermine the kind of extremely sophisticated attack such as the one that suspected Iranian-linked hackers were caught engaging in through early 2019, which relied on subtly redirecting traffic to help steal login credentials from high-value targets.

It would also thwart much cruder DNS attacks and sabotages, which while far less sophisticated and thought through than the Iran-style targeted attacks, are much more publicly chaotic and demonstrate the risks much more obviously.

One of the most dramatic such attacks to date was in 2016, and was at the time the largest ever distributed denial of service attack (DDoS) ever seen, by quite some margin[6] – several years on it is still the second-largest recorded attack, and the largest one that can be said to have succeeded.

A DDoS attack is really clever and really straightforward at the same time. The clever bit is that it relies on compromising thousands or even millions of online devices at once, and then using all of them to attack another system. This means if an attacker can get a virus or worm that spreads very rapidly – ideally without even needing an unwary user to click the wrong attachment – you will have lots of computers ready to use to attack someone.

In the case of the 2016 attack against the DNS system, this clever bit was done using 'Internet of Things' devices, a term describing adding non-traditional computers like TV set-top boxes, video cameras, speakers, baby monitors and more to the internet. These typically have much worse security (and are much harder to update) that computers and mobiles.

Once the attacker has their network of compromised devices – usually called a 'botnet' – they can do the easy and stupid bit: they tell all of the devices, all at once, to try to load content from one site, or one server, again and again. The attack in question focused on Dyn, one of the companies at the core of the DNS system.

Despite only attacking one of several companies integral to the service, this relatively crude attack took down thousands of sites for millions of users across the world, for hours at a time.

Unlike attacks which target their own systems, there is nothing the administrators of affected websites can do: anyone who knows the website's IP address could type it in and visit the page just fine – their servers are working! – but how many sites have you memorised the IP address for? If you're anything like a normal user, it's zero.

In the long run, the Dyn attack wasn't particularly scary: the company dealt with it within twenty-four hours, and it didn't become a new normal. Disconcertingly, though, not only did no one ever work out who was behind the attack, they also never found out any solid reasons why the attack had taken place. For such a crude attempt, that's hardly reassuring.

ICANN and its stakeholders have clearly managed to think up a new and more secure system that would fix at least some of the system's problems, and they still host regular ceremonies to keep its certificates up to date; but nearly a decade after the system began, it's still barely used in practice, even if the big players have signed up in theory.

'Slow and bureaucratic' are supposedly dead concepts, things of the past when it comes to the 'move fast and break things' mantras of the Silicon Valley start-ups – but when it comes to online infrastructure, the analogy seems to be more 'move fast, grow fast, fix achingly slowly'.

The struggles of working out these tensions are more obvious in what – at first at least – seems like one of ICANN's more trivial functions: deciding what gets to be a web domain, and who gets to administer it if so.

There are different rules over who is eligible or not to buy different web addresses: .com was initially intended to be for commercial use only, but was then opened up to general use and so anyone in any country can buy a domain if they can afford it and it's available. Other domains have tighter criteria: .edu can only be used by US educational establishments, .ac.uk is

UK academia only. Meanwhile .eu can only be registered by EU nationals, and .cat is solely for the use of the Catalan community.

It's ICANN that gets to decide who administers each of these top-level domains (TLDs), and they often decide between competing bids – for example, a company wanting to sell .cat to moggie fanciers will have had to compete with Catalonia. In many cases, this is simple: countries tend to get first refusal, and also companies that wish to register their trademark as a TLD – Google has done this (handy if users forget to type .com, as it means 'www.google', which once would have led to an error, now works), as has BMW, and others.

These are not always so uncontentious: what about when your brand name is also, for example, the name of the world's largest rainforest? The result is a bitter and years-long row, which has also ended up dragging in more and more countries – we might have views on .amazon in English, but what about the symbols in Chinese or Japanese? Who owns those – the business or the people living in the South American region? All of this ends up on Marby's desk.

'There is no international trademark law,' he says. 'We have to deal with trademark things because ... well, my favourite right now is who owns the word Amazon? We are right now in the middle of it and they're not happy. We have decided to come up with a way where we share the delegation between real representatives of the people in the Amazonian region and the company. That's what we want to do, and only ICANN can come up with something like that. The funny thing is that Amazon has the trademark in some of those countries. People come together and try to solve a problem. The fact that some of those South American countries now seem to disagree with themselves is another problem. They really don't like me right now.'

Resolving who gets the snappier .amazon online address might seem much lower stakes than keeping traffic on the internet flowing, and preventing it being intercepted by bad actors – but it shows up in the same way how far ahead the internet has got versus law and versus regulation.

There exists no legal basis to settle the dispute: trademark law isn't sufficiently advanced internationally to give a preference one way or the other. That means there's no court or parliament in existence to adjudicate the decision formally. As Marby notes, not even the UN could adjudicate it, had they chosen to, because there's no legal basis to any of it – just ICANN butting heads together and trying to muddle through.

Critics of ICANN do tend to flag on this particular point that the not-for-profit does quite well out of managing this part of the system – in 2018, it had just under $100 million in revenue from expanding the domain system, plus a further $240 million from auctioning off popular top-level domains – and it receives around $130 million a year in income from the registrars who sell domain names to the public, as tech site *The Register* reported.[7] Some headaches pay better than others.

Overall, though, Marby talks more like someone holding together a system which no one had really planned, and which no one had really expected to take off in the way that it did.

'I think that the notion of getting people connected was the utopian thing,' he says. 'The disruption of our business models, all of that, that was not part of the plan. I can probably prove that because then most of them would have actually started companies if they'd foreseen that. They didn't, because nobody saw it coming.'

DNS IS HARDLY the only crucial internet protocol that's based on something designed in the 1980s and bodged and revised ever since, as the internet grew from a few thousand devices to billions.

Another of the fundamental technologies that makes the internet work – and without which the network of networks would fail – was quite literally drawn up on the back of a napkin.

Or to be exact, three napkins[8] – photocopies of which are still on display in Cisco's archives, as the original napkins were long lost to the rubbish bin, even as the ideas jotted on them continue to power key global infrastructure.[9] The napkins were the result of a meeting between a Cisco engineer and an IBM engineer at an internet conference in 1989, the same year the World Wide Web was conceived.

The internet at this point was already starting to creak, and needed better ways to transmit its data – DNS might be there, handling which written addresses corresponded to which IPs, but the network also needed to know which routers were physically connected to which other routers: where were the actual cables and connections?

The 'three napkin' protocol the two engineers threw together, also known as Border Gateway Protocol (BGP), was about finding physical routes between two spots on the network. One very rough way to think of the two protocols is that DNS is the online version of a phone book, giving you the connections between people's names and their phone number. BGP, on the other hand, much more closely resembles your satnav – it tells you what routes are available to you once you've decided where you're going.[10]

The men were looking to fix the immediate problems causing headaches on the network. They were not building a scalable idea that would make sense decades later. The napkins served as a good signal of that.

So, the protocol they developed is of course the one still in use across the internet today – working, as ever, from thrown-together-proposal, to Request For Comment, to a protocol refined over a few years and finalised in 1994 and (so far) never replaced.[11]

'Short-term solutions tend to stay with us for a very long time. And long-term solutions tend to never happen,' Yakov Rekhter, the IBM engineer behind BGP told the *Washington Post* in 2015. 'That's what I learned from this experience.'

Within the multi-billion-dollar private companies that rely on the internet, and encourage us to move ever more of our lives there, security and protocols are rebuilt seemingly overnight – with teams of the world's most skilled and best-paid engineers orchestrating hugely complex database migrations, server moves and ultra-fast infrastructure.

In the space in between those enterprises, the contrast couldn't be more marked: for a mixture of politics, legal liability and inertia, nothing happens – and so we have a series of protocols designed for an internet of a different generation by people who never imagined they'd be left in service for so long. And we're left to face the consequences of that inaction.

One man who knows this system better than most is Tom Daly, the senior vice president for infrastructure at Fastly, a company which provides online services to try to improve page-load times for internet companies, and reduce the load and cost on its servers (among other services).

Daly has to understand BGP to avoid accidentally knocking out some of the internet's key servers: because they manage so much traffic, Fastly has to spread it around.

'You can see our home page right now, we're processing about eight million requests per second at a state of over five terabits of traffic per second out to the internet,' he explains.[12] 'I don't believe that there is one ISP that we could hand all of our traffic to and say, "Hey, Mr ISP, go deliver all this traffic to end-user networks for us."'

Daly tries to set out how BGP works in principle, and links it to the idea of airport transponders: it's not like being able to see a whole, huge map of the internet in front of you, he says. What you can see is your near neighbours signalling who they are, and some of the places they can route traffic towards.

'One of the ways that you can think of BGP is as the homing beacon protocol for the internet. So if you think about how planes fly and how they navigate and how they find airports, you have all these homing beacons all over the earth, they're at airports, they're at navigation holds and all they do is emit a radio signal.'

The different thing with BGP is that it also echoes down the line the other connections near to it – a bit like a plane flying across the Atlantic picking up Heathrow's beacon, and hearing Heathrow also shouting, 'Hey, you can also come via me for Schiphol, Paris, Edinburgh, Brussels and Rome.'

That same plane might be picking up the transmitter from Paris as well, letting it know 'you can travel via me for Heathrow, Schiphol, Brussels, Madrid and Rome'. The plane is left with the knowledge that there are multiple routes, and what they are – even if it doesn't know what the best of them might be.

The whole BGP system is even more decentralised than DNS – there's no 'root' zone to it, there's not really any particular board overseeing it or acting as a clearing house, though major servers near the core infrastructure of the internet do have, in practice, a louder voice in the system than others.

On a standard day, BGP helps an immensely complex network keep its traffic moving, marrying together the physical and logical infrastructures of the internet.

As systems engineer Ben Cox notes, BGP isn't neutral – what signals which routes is a result of both the political and financial relationships that govern the day-to-day functioning of the network.

'Obviously, the world is not as beautiful as we want it to be,' he says, explaining that networks will generally only peer with each other when there's either money in it for them or mutual benefit to be had, such as if their customers' traffic needs the other company's network too. 'No one runs networks for the sake of it. Networks, fundamentally, have a commercial interest.'

The result is that looking at BGP, and who's connected to whom, is more revealing than you might think.

'I think it's beautiful … it's like 780,000 routes of political decisions, decisions that people have made. Some of them are normal decisions like, "You're just a customer, you're paying money. I'm going to give you this." Others are more interesting. If you look at Africa's internet market, one of the interesting things you find is, I guess the better way says, routing isn't really ever derived by logic. Logic is not really a part of BGP because, ultimately, people don't really follow logic.

'There are two things that drive BGP routing: inter-geographical politics and money. Money is just money, it's everywhere, but the politics bit is really interesting. If you look at the African internet market, obviously a lot of African countries were previously colonies. You can very easily spot who used to own a country because the national telecom in the colonial country will route through the owning country first. So British colonies will build connections to Britain first as their primary platform to the rest of the world, and likewise French colonies will build connections into France. This is because they originally laid down the telephone network. The relationships were there and there's no real point in changing it, right?'

Networks are never neutral – and so even something so apparently technical and practical as BGP reveals power relationships in its day-to-day operation. Engineers didn't deliberately decide to set up their BGP to reflect these twentieth-century relationships – it just fell naturally out of their existing connections, and thus replicated and continued them into a new era.

And that's when things are working to plan. The problem, in the twenty-first century when not every player is honest and when the internet is critical infrastructure, is that at its core the system is built entirely on trust. Daly finds it easiest to continue with his plane analogy to explain the theory of this trick – though it turns out not to be an especially complicated attack.

Basically, Daly says, if someone is sitting on the internet with BGP enabled – maybe they're a regional internet service provider, or similar – there is almost nothing stopping you just suddenly declaring that you offer routes to whatever you like, whether it's true or not.

'That's like Heathrow airport suddenly deciding to say "Hey, on my beacons I'm going to say that I'm Boston", and all these planes for Boston start showing up. That can happen in BGP.'

If that sounds like it would be a bad idea in aviation, it's also a bad idea on the internet, albeit with less immediately spectacular (and calamitous) results. One of the earlier incidents that brought the potential havoc of BGP hijacking – this kind of false declaration – to public attention was what was intended to be a low-key effort by Pakistan to censor a YouTube video, for reportedly containing material insulting to Muslims.[13]

'There is some content on YouTube that is offensive to the Pakistani government for whatever reason,' Daly recounts. 'So the Pakistani government goes to the ISPs in Pakistan and says, "There's this content. We're censoring it. We don't want people accessing it."'

Pakistan Telecom decided to comply with the order, which ordered one specific video URL and three IPs to be blocked, by 'blackholing' them – updating its BGP table to direct anyone asking for those to go down a non-existent cable (or a loop) so that the site would just show as being unavailable.

The ISP did two things wrong, though: first, it didn't just block the specified video, it blocked out the entirety of YouTube (though some reports suggest Pakistani authorities had intentionally widened their original order). Second – and what brought the issue to global attention – Pakistan Telecom didn't just shout the news about its fake new route to its own customers, it also shouted about this new route to some of the bigger global ISPs it dealt with.

'I forget who the upstream transit provider was [it was a Hong Kong ISP], but they accepted that routing update,' Daly says. 'Then they echoed that onto their peers. Eventually, it propagated through a significant portion of the internet. Because each person, each place is going to get it from somewhere they decided to trust as well.'

Thanks to that daisy chain of trust, almost all of the world's major ISPs came to believe that the new and primary route to YouTube was via Pakistan Telecom – and as soon as any of the signals reached that ISP, they were thrown into the black hole. The result was for YouTube to appear down across most of the world, despite no attack touching its own servers in any way whatsoever.

'That's an example of a classic misconfiguration causing a black hole on the internet,' Daly explains. 'One of the problems with BGP is that it's a gossip-based protocol. If you're playing the game telephone with your friends, what happens to the message as it gets down to the end of the line? It's a mess. That can happen with these BGP announcements.'

Blackholing is not the only risk of BGP hijacking, though it's obviously a serious one. Another is tactically redirecting traffic while still letting it reach its intended destination. Nation states and other sophisticated actors are able to get significant information on traffic if they can make it cross a network they control, either by intercepting the fibre-optic cable and saving its output, or by analysing it in near-real time using a technique called deep packet inspection.

This kind of technique could be used, hypothetically, by a country such as China to reroute traffic on the other side of the world to travel via cables and networks under its control – perhaps with the goal of stealing industrial secrets. This would add so little extra time to the process that it would be virtually unnoticeable even by corporations with advanced security procedures, and the routing information could be reversed when the attack wasn't active, becoming all but invisible.

As a result, it's perhaps unsurprising that when November 2018 traffic to millions of IP addresses operated by Google suddenly re-routed via China – taking out services for Google users and other companies using its cloud-based products – suspicions were high: was China engaging in some low-scale information warfare via a well-known vulnerability?

In that particular case, the hunch was no – the evidence pointed towards cock-up rather than conspiracy, via the mechanism of a Nigerian internet service provider updating its BGP policies and tables by hand, and someone during the process making an error which suddenly caused large-scale disruption for one of the world's biggest companies, and very nearly an international incident.[14]

These are hardly isolated occurrences. In December 2017, suspicions were raised when traffic destined for Facebook, Microsoft, Google, Apple and others was briefly re-routed – for around three minutes at a time – via Russia, in a move which would have represented a test of a proof-of-concept attack (or could have been a mistake, of course).[15] In April 2018, an attacker managed to re-route a selection of IP addresses operated by an Amazon service and use them to defraud people of around $150,000 in cryptocurrencies.[16] And in that July, a day before the country was due to be hit by street protests, traffic for the popular encrypted messaging app Telegram was re-routed via Iran.[17]

The YouTube/Pakistan incident is now more than ten years in the past, and nothing has changed with BGP, and nothing seems likely to. Major incidents centring on either BGP mistakes or blatant misuse now emerge every few months, and could easily already have resulted in the interception of sensitive messages, or the theft of major intellectual property: if such attacks are done subtly, they never even come to garner the niche headlines they currently get.

The security flaws are inherent to the protocol – and yet there seems to be next to zero public alarm.

'It is real,' Daly says. 'If you're a malicious actor who can essentially get unconstrained rights to announce prefixes into the global routing system at the right locations, some real damage can occur. Because think about it, and go back to the DNS as the example. Everyone was scared that traffic could be directed to a destination that wasn't the real place. I'm going to put up a phishing website that looks like, in my case, Bank of America ... If I can put up a page that is impersonating that bank, and I can trick the DNS in descending the user there, I get usernames, I get passwords, I get social security numbers, whatever it might be. Maybe I make some transfers on our behalf and we get rich. That's famously true of BGP. I don't have to trick the control plane of the internet into sending traffic to the wrong place. I'm just going to assert that I am the place the traffic should naturally go to by definition. If you're not looking at monitoring what's going on in BGP, how do you actually detect that it's a hijack?'

The vulnerabilities of the system he created are hardly lost on Yakov Rekhter, either. But the problem, as he noted in his *Washington Post* interview, is that the internet grew up faster than its governance.

'There is a cost associated with doing security. And the question is: Who is going to pay the price?' he said. 'Unless operators can see that the benefits will generally outweigh the costs, they just won't deploy it.'

Because no one is in line to get the blame, no one is taking responsibility.

THE US IS famously the richest country in the world: it is a statement of pride, something proclaimed on the stump speech of politicians from presidents down to local town halls.

It's also a country with a guilty secret: its infrastructure is crumbling. Around two-thirds of the USA's roads are classified as in 'dire need' of repair, while around one in eleven bridges are flagged as in serious need of repair.[18] The country's water system is ageing and under-invested, costing households and businesses hundreds of billions in losses and damages.[19] The water in the city of Flint, Michigan, has been left undrinkable for more than four years, due to lead poisoning after switching to a cheaper water source.[20]

This extends to the physical infrastructure of the US internet: the USA has some of the slowest broadband speeds in the developed world, it has one of the slowest roll-outs of fast internet – with huge numbers unable to access it at all – and its consumers are charged among the most for that inadequate service.[21]

The USA is clearly not too poor to improve its infrastructure – either it has decided it can tolerate the risk of ageing and creaking infrastructure, or its politics have failed in repairing them.

Should it really, then, be a surprise that the internet has come to so closely mirror the country which shaped so much of its early development? The internet has made billionaires out of hundreds of its pioneers, and enriched plenty of their rich early supporters still further.

Like the US, it has become integral to global commerce and an undeniable force on the world stage. And like the US, its institutions seem weak and underfunded, and with almost no prospect of being improved – while the private sector has flourished beyond most people's wildest dreams, the public space has withered on the vine, paralysed by inaction and mistrust, a lack of funding, a lack of imagination and a lack of liability.

The custodians of these public elements of the internet are not bad people – they are far from it, receiving far less money than many of their counterparts in the private sector, and grimly fighting their often grindingly slow losing battles. It's easy to see romance in it, a David versus Goliath face-off.

But when these aren't biblical, Goliath tends to win – and in this instance it's not even one fight: as noted earlier, it's a need to rebuild a spaceship while out in the cold vacuum, ideally without bothering any of the passengers. While that's phenomenally difficult, and beyond the resources and attention paid so far, it's surely not beyond the collective imagination of Silicon Valley – if the considerable resources they have at their disposal are brought to bear on it.

The internet is the cornerstone of the global economy, and the bedrock it's built on was designed to support a small experimental network. The castle is not so much built on sand as right there on the water – just as dotcom founders drive $250,000 Tesla Roadsters over crumbling roads, so too are their businesses relying on fundamentally broken online infrastructure.

Rebuilding it won't be easy, but it will only get more difficult the longer it's put off. The big question is: who can make the people who have benefited most from the internet dig in to fix the system that made their fortunes? Can anyone?

MY MIND TURNS back to ICANN chief executive Göran Marby, and the 'off button' his friend bought for him. For Marby, the button seems to cheer him, to remind him he provides a service and people choose to use it.

'We are not part of the infrastructure side,' he says. 'We contribute with a logic that is used and people have chosen to use it. ISPs have chosen to use it. That's what we provide. Physically, ICANN as an organisation has no button to push.'

It's not a nondescript button – it's an elevated red plunger that would not look out of place on any TV sci-fi's control panel.

As our interview concludes, I ask Marby straight out – what actually happens if you push the button?

He smiles. 'Try it.'

I push the button. There's a quiet, disappointing click.

Then nothing. I leave.

Part Two
THE MONEY

4

The Money Men

IF YOU WERE going to imagine an office designed to host some of the internet's hottest start-ups, betaworks's[1] New York studio would be almost exactly what you'd picture. We're in New York's fashionable Meatpacking District, surrounded by designer shops, restaurants and bars, and just yards from the Hudson River.

As you walk into the building you're greeted with a wall of some of the biggest successes of the crowdfunding site Kickstarter, in which betaworks invested. There is a prototype Oculus Rift VR headset ($2.4 million raised), Hickies no-tie shoelaces ($580,000 raised), the Light Phone, an ultra-minimalist mobile phone ($415,000), and Sammy Screamer, a mobile alarm to 'keep an eye on your stuff' ($90,840), all on show as I visit.

In the reception to the huge open-plan space, replete with the expected kitchens, chill-out areas, ultra-modern seating and more, you can catch snippets of conversation which also sound exactly like a tech investment company should. 'Some would say a BuzzFeed, a version of BuzzFeed,' says a man on an intense phone call, who's paying little regard to being in a public area. 'They have a nice dashboard they've used to figure out what works, a few channels on Facebook ...' he continues, as his pitch drifts off into the middle distance.

Betaworks is a 'start-up studio' and an early-stage investor in some of the biggest names on the internet. It has invested in

Twitter, in part through two companies who were eventually bought out by Twitter,[2] Tumblr, and a number of other companies that make up the social internet. These have included bit.ly, the URL shortener (more important when web addresses counted towards your Twitter character limit) and analytics tool, and Giphy, the online gif repository now built into a number of social media tools.

In addition to its Kickstarter investment, betaworks also backed the blogging network Medium (founded by Twitter co-founder Evan Williams) and the podcasting company Gimlet Media (now owned by Spotify).[3] It's also funded numerous analytics companies used by social media businesses and content creators, and even built the hit iPhone and Android games Dots and Two Dots, before spinning those out as a separate company.[4]

The way betaworks operates is by investing in companies when they're still very small – sometimes taking them into their studios when they might still only have a handful of people (often the co-founders) working for them, and haven't raised any money yet. In other instances, betaworks invests when companies are at what's called the 'seed' stages of venture capital.

Such investments are high risk and high return: the money is put in long before the company is a safe bet, and exactly when it might yet still be beaten out by one or several would-be rivals, or else simply fizzle out. Venture capital funds that work in this way invest less money in each company – investing in companies later down the line can mean spending tens or hundreds of millions at a time – but make more bets.

If, then, it seems strange that one investment company has played a role in the development of so many household names on the internet – companies between them with hundreds of millions of users across the world – that's just how the internet works.

The general law of the internet is that you don't try to grow a profitable business from day one: you concentrate on getting big first – taking advantage of the benefits of scale and of building up users as fast as possible – and worry about making money later. That means that for the first several years of operating, you need new investment to keep going, and that means you need specialist investors.

And this is where the venture capital (VC) firms come in – investment companies that typically specialise in internet companies (often of one particular type, like social, analytics, big data, biomedical or something else) and which end up cross-pollinating the way tech companies work from one to another. This can mean corporate culture, but also business model, board members and more. If we want to understand how the internet got like it has now – and who wins or loses from that – understanding where the money comes from, and who takes the profit, is essential.

That's what brings me to betaworks, and to its founder John Borthwick, who insists betaworks doesn't work like a typical VC operation, and whose willingness to meet me suggests he may have a point. He proudly notes on the way to our meeting room that he was a witness against Microsoft during the company's US competition case in 2000, which briefly saw a judge order the business split in two. Borthwick stops as he tells this story to show me a sketch from the court artist on the day of his testimony, which hangs in the betaworks offices.

Borthwick, a former Time Warner executive who then ran his own start-up, has thus been on the other side of answering to investors, and coping with what can seem like their odd and rigid demands.

'I've been an entrepreneur,' he says. 'I've built companies, sold companies, grown companies up, broken companies, helped to make companies, and I thought that the instrument of VC was a fairly crude instrument that did one or two things really well but, in the process, did a whole bunch of things not so well.'

Borthwick then proceeds to illustrate his initially diplomatically made point more sharply, reflecting on his own experience as the CEO of a start-up.

'One of the things which I've learned, and I've learned a lot about VC, is when I was running a company called Fotolog, which was a very large photo-sharing site in the early days of Facebook. It was a pre-Flickr before Flickr and it grew very large outside the United States.'

The site, which at the time billed itself as the 'largest photo-blogging community' and the 'third most-trafficked social media network', had by 2007 secured itself 11 million users and 300 million photos had been uploaded.[5] As a result – given the burgeoning success of Facebook and Twitter at the time – buyers were circling. But at first, at least, investors assured Borthwick they were in it for the long run.

'I was an angel investor [a fairly early-stage investor who typically puts in less than $1 million] in the company. I then left Time Warner and stepped in to run the company. I got some interest in the company being acquired. I went to our investors, our VC investors, and said, "Do you want to sell?" They were like, "Absolutely not, we're committed to just being with this company. Absolutely not." The first offer was for twenty million.'

With twenty million dollars on the table, Borthwick's financial backers told him they were on his side, with him for the long haul, and not interested in selling the company for a quick buck. He could rest easy ... couldn't he?

INVESTMENT – LIKE EVERY other important element of what really matters online – is buried in its own jargon, but at the core of it are ideas that are obvious as soon as you stop to think about them. If you want to build a business in the real world, it's fairly straightforward to do so: let's imagine you'd like to build a restaurant.

You need to raise enough money to cover a lease, fit the place out and the early costs of staff (this can be quite a lot of money), but in theory at least you will be aiming to cover your operating costs almost from the get-go – once you've got that initial funding, that should be all you need, at least for quite some time. If your restaurant is profitable, you might then after a few years expand to a second site. If it's very successful and you're ambitious, at that point you might go to investors to try to take a gamble and expand *fast*. You can aim to build a small business, a medium one or a large one – whichever you prefer, and whichever works for you.

For a whole host of reasons, online just doesn't seem to work that way. Part of this is intrinsic to the internet: if you open a new restaurant, you're mainly competing with other restaurants in the same street or neighbourhood, and perhaps slightly competing with other restaurants in the same town.

If you launch a new online-only business, you're competing with every other business doing something similar in the whole world – including ones that may see your good idea and try to copy it. If you want to grow slowly and steadily, developing features as you can and living within your means, while your copycat rival is willing to operate at a loss and take investment – and so becomes able to develop features faster, advertise more, and so on – they will quickly supplant you. If your service becomes inferior, can you really trust your users to stick with you when switching is as easy as a click?

Perhaps even more important is the sense of an online gold rush, though: why try to build a small business that might eventually make you a few tens or hundreds of thousands of dollars in profit each year when seemingly all around you, you can see companies selling for hundreds of millions – if not billions?

The result of that is most dotcom start-ups choose to follow the VC money: grow as fast as you can, trying at each stage to up your valuation and get larger and larger sums of investment, not worrying too much about revenues until several rounds into the process. The result means handing large shares of the company – and usually, with a few exceptions, a large degree of control – to investors, in the hope of making it big.

The phases of the process break down like this:[6] start-ups initially bootstrap themselves – in the sense of 'pulling yourself up by your bootstraps', and with the same self-satisfied implication that anyone who makes it big in tech has done it thanks to their own talents, because in the earliest days of their start-up they used their own savings, lived frugally, worked out of their mum's garage, etc., to get their company going.

The next phase of funding is the friends and family round, which is exactly what it sounds like: people tapping up their personal networks, usually for a sum in the tens of thousands of dollars, often to hire a first developer or some other specialist service that can't be got for free or for favours.

If it seems like bootstrapping and friends and family rounds provide severe barriers for anyone who doesn't come from a comfortable upper-middle-class background in becoming a dotcom start-up, that's precisely because they do. Inequality starts very early when it comes to the financing of the internet.

It's at this stage that professional investors begin to get involved, if the company has something to it. The first round at which an investor like John Borthwick might get involved is as an angel investor, someone who invests when the company is still at a very early stage – likely still with a young and inexperienced management team – and so expects to give a good deal of their time as well as their money to the company.

Angels can often end up running the companies they invest in, as happened with Borthwick and Fotolog. Sums involved at this stage still tend to be small, often below $100,000 or so. Angel investing is seen as distinct from venture capital in the industry, but many well-known VCs often make angel investments in a personal capacity, using their own money. Venture capital has been intrinsically tied up with technology and with the internet for as long as either has existed – the concept developed in the US post-war investments, supported the birth of Silicon Valley and hit the big time with the first dotcom boom.

Where VCs start to get involved formally is at the seed round of funding, a stage that marks the professionalisation of the company and a sign it's about to get onto riding the VC tiger until an exit, one way or another. This round can range from a few tens of thousands of dollars up to around a million or so – and by this stage a founder could easily have given away up to a third or more of the equity in their business.

With that kind of stake, and with the ability to impose various other requirements thanks to holding the purse strings, VCs from this point become hard to ignore for all but the most confident founders of the most successful start-ups – the Zuckerbergs of the world.

Companies may go through several more rounds of raising VC funding from this point – a sign that even five or more years after being founded they are still reliant on investors' cash to operate. Series A funding is usually in the low seven figures, with Series B coming a few years later and typically being in the region of $10 million plus.

For large companies that need lots of money to operate, Series C funding can easily be $50 million to hundreds of millions. This is the kind of money you need if you're something like Deliveroo[7] or Uber[8], companies which grow by subsidising the cost of the service they provide: if you're going to charge customers less than the cost to you of offering it, someone has to put up that cash, after all.

VC funds do this to seek an exit: either selling the start-up to a bigger tech company, or else an initial public offering – listing the company's shares publicly on the stock exchange. Before that point, everyone investing has had to be invited to do so by the company, and VCs secure privileged access to funding rounds through a trick of making it a condition of early-stage funding to get better access if the company gets to Series B and Series C – letting them lock up the potential upsides of big bets later with a small amount of cash in seed rounds.

This generally means that when it comes to start-ups, the institutional investors who can invest early get most of the upside: by the time the company actually goes public – when you or I could invest – its valuation is already sky-high. The rich get richer. The flipside of this is that unlike buying a stock in a public company – which you can sell any time you like – investing in start-ups ties up your money. VCs want a large return in a relatively short period of time, to return profits to their fund's investors.

That means that if it doesn't look like an initial public offering, or some other exit for a huge sum, is forthcoming then VCs will very quickly shift their slide rule in favour of a sale, as Borthwick learned.

When Borthwick had first been approached with a $20 million offer for Fotolog in 2007, his investors had told him 'absolutely not, we're committed' for the long run. But when the offer went up, what he was told changed, fast.

'We ended up two months later selling it for about 90 million,' Borthwick says. 'The seminal moment was when I got to an offer for about 75 million. The VCs had said no at 70, and at 75, they were like, "Sell. Right now." I was like, "There's a spreadsheet behind this, isn't there …?" I was like, "This smells like an algorithm." Sure enough, they have a return analysis that they do.'

In other words, as the founder of a company – or the person who's currently its CEO – it's possible that you might want to keep going as an independent, but find the fate of your business decided by an Excel spreadsheet run by one of your investors, who is restricted by the expectations of the people who in turn fund them.

'VC money also has a very specific investment life associated with it,' Borthwick continues. 'Five years typically. Because of that, it's again like a scalpel. It's like it really works well for certain things, but you certainly don't want to use it for another purpose that it's not well suited for. I think there are many companies who are going to end up being very successful companies but outside of that time frame. The VCs within that time frame will say, "Well, we need to get our money back. We'll optimise for some optimal return or optimise for an early exit, or earlier exit, because our business model requires it."'

One effect of this intense and rigid funding model – and the growth model it not so much encourages as requires – is that companies can essentially find themselves needing to match the growth and revenue necessary to justify it, and keep the eagle-eyed investors onside.

The money you accept from an investor effectively sets the valuation of your company, and starts you along a ratchet. If you accept, say, $50,000 of angel investment for 12.5 per cent of your company, you now have a company with a valuation of $400,000.[9] But now there is an expectation from your new investor that within a year or two you will be able to raise several hundred thousand at a valuation of several million – and onwards, and upwards.

This is all fine until suddenly your company's growth doesn't match what investors expect, or if you're suddenly expected to raise revenues – and it's here that the connection between the VC model and some of the most common concerns about the internet becomes apparent.

If you have to demonstrate growth in active users and the amount of time they spend on your service to survive, then you will test and re-test every bit of your service to maximise those, trying to keep users on your app, site or service as long as possible – the accusation levelled against Facebook (among other services) by its co-founder Sean Parker, when he said the service was designed to be addictive.[10]

And if the selling points of your business to existing and would-be investors is the huge size of your user base, how much you know about their interests and how long they spend on your service, then the obvious route to monetising those things is through the privacy-invading targeted adverts that became the business model of the internet.

It's a point Borthwick acknowledges, upon reflection, when I push him on it during our interview.

'I think, again it's going back to that finely edged scalpel, that finely pointed scalpel ...' he says. 'One of the things that you can do with VC financing is that if you're on the right side of a growth momentum curve you can raise extraordinary amounts of money. I have seen companies, in our portfolio and outside of betaworks, raise too much money ... you specifically point towards programmatic or attention-based monetisation as being the fastest solution to a question of "How am I going to monetise now I've raised a couple of hundred million dollars and I've made a dime?"'

He pauses, before continuing slowly and carefully.

'I think the VC is definitely part of that toxic or that potentially toxic mix.'

There are inherent tensions built into VC, too: on one level, they're based on the idea of getting rich by backing the scrappy upstart against big and well-established companies, but on the other, they often either founded several of those bigger companies and invested in them, or else they work with other partners who did the same.

They also often make their money by steering new start-ups towards a bigger company in their sector which buys them up. Sometimes these purchases are just interest expansion, sometimes they're a way of hiring a talented team working on something that could be a product for the bigger business – such as Twitter buying Tweetdeck, an interface for its social network – but sometimes they're a way of buying up a potential rival to protect your own business, a practice which Facebook has repeatedly been accused of with its acquisition of WhatsApp.[11]

The result of internet giants' willingness to swallow the young firms who might supplant them – and of VCs' willingness to take the paydays that go with letting that happen – is an end to the era of full-scale innovation, Borthwick suggests.

'This incredible innovation comes along, but then these big guys just buy it. It's like the innovation cycle's also been hampered by this. I remember going to a website and it was just all about possibility and creativity and trying new things and so on, and it's just got very narrow. I think on the internet today, most of the interesting stuff is pretty hard to find or is happening off the internet.'

It is a rare company that emerges as an online giant without going through the venture capital process, and so a rare company that doesn't become hit by its many side effects – effects we all live with daily as we use social networks designed to maximise and monetise our attention spans. There is a twist worth noting at this stage, though, which is that VCs aren't quite as much of a bubble as they can seem.

It's easy to think of VC as its own world with its own (arguably toxic) culture, and in many ways it is: most of the top VCs are the internet entrepreneurs of the last generation. Marc Andreessen was a co-founder of Netscape, then became a top VC funding Facebook, Skype, Twitter, and more. Peter Thiel co-founded

PayPal, then became Facebook's first outside investor, and now funds much more. There are many others we could name.

But they are not only investing their own money – they might well be investing yours, as Brian O'Kelley, an advertising tech executive and investor (who speaks at length next chapter), notes. It's 'limited partners' – investment funds, university endowments, pension funds and more – that are putting the money into VC firms, and they're the ones demanding big returns to keep their funds in the black.

'Go one level above the VC, go to the limited partners, the endowments and the pension funds that are funding the VCs,' O'Kelley says. 'Are we willing to instruct those VCs to make ethics the priority over returns? This is interesting, because the VCs are just another middleman. If Princeton's endowment says, "We're going to get 14 per cent returns, because that return goes into paying for education and education is the greatest social good," then maybe the ends justify the means ... Do we need to have a better conversation through the whole system? Honestly, if you said to Princeton, or Harvard, or the New York State Pension Fund, "What are the instructions you're giving these VCs? Or what are the criteria of hiring fund managers?" 99 per cent of the time, it's on absolute return. That, to me, is the root of the problem.'

Venture capital is the ultimate group of insiders – the dotcom winners of one generation picking the winners of the next, backing them with their own money and with the money of established and respected investors. So much control is put in so few hands because the system, so far anyway, seems to work – in financial terms, at least. And for a long time, it's felt safe to only focus on those because the internet was the home of the upstarts and the disruptors; it's only now, as we start to accept the internet businesses *are* the incumbents, that the need for more reflection on the business and funding model, and perhaps the need to slow down, becomes clear.

It's a tension Borthwick – whose very studio, betaworks, is built off and named after a culture of experimentation, trying things out (of 'betas'), and moving fast – does now acknowledge. Times have changed.

'I think that culture of move fast and break things or fuck it, ship it, and just get it out, has been a large contributor to some of the unintended consequences that we've seen today.'

VCs aren't trusted with so much money and power over the online ecosystem for nothing: they often have an insight into what the internet is doing to the world long ahead of the rest of us – even if their main motivation for looking into it is using that insight to make money.

Take Albert Wenger, now a managing partner at Union Square Ventures (USV), one of the most successful venture capital firms of recent years, with billion-dollar exits for seven years running from 2011.[12] USV considers itself a relatively small fund, which invests early – at seed or Series A – in around twenty to twenty-five companies per fund it raises (VCs create 'funds' with a group of investors and a certain amount of capital, with a plan on when to exit and return the money), builds its investment in the winners in subsequent rounds until it hits 15 per cent to 20 per cent, then seeks an exit.

'Getting *valued* at a billion or more does nothing for our model,' a 2017 blogpost by one of the firm's partners noted. 'We need these high impact companies to *exit* at a billion dollars or more.' (Emphasis added.)

The company seeks to get those exits within about seven or eight years – considered a long investment in the VC world, but one explained by its preference for early-stage investments.

Wenger came to the VC game in a very similar way to Borthwick: he was president of del.icio.us, a service to share bookmarked websites (and so a precursor to Twitter and similar services), and then an angel investor in craft site Etsy and the social network Tumblr.[13] USV currently invests in Soundcloud, Kickstarter, Stripe (a payments service), Foursquare and duolingo. It has exited investments including Twitter, Tumblr, Etsy and Zynga (maker of Farmville).[14]

But Wenger's ability to spot what was coming, he tells me from the corner office of USV's nineteenth-storey offices in Manhattan, just yards from the Flatiron Building, pre-dated most of the internet boom by a long way. It started from the first time he tinkered with the web – just four years after its 1989 invention.

'I distinctly recall the first time I discovered the web,' Wenger says. 'It was in '93. I was at MIT. I was supposedly doing my stats homework at the time. We still went to computer rooms with workstations to do stats. I was trying to focus on my stats assignment. This person next to me was, click, look, click, something new on the screen, click, look, laugh. Click. I'm like, "What are you doing?" He was like, "Well, I'm surfing the web." "What is that?" He's like, "Well, this is a thing on your workstation now called Mosaic. Why don't you try that out?"… Then of course instead of doing my stats, I spent the next four hours surfing the web … It was just random pages by random people. A bunch of MIT pages that led you to a bunch of other pages. What I remember most was walking home on a really cold Cambridge night and thinking, "Oh my God, newspapers are totally screwed." I was convinced this was going to happen so quickly. Then it took twenty years to play itself out.'

Today, that insight might seem a statement of the obvious. In 1993, it was an almost revolutionary insight – the *New York Times* didn't launch any online presence until 1996, the BBC had nothing until 1997, and the *Guardian*'s online presence didn't launch until 1999, and at first all were seen as sideshows versus the main event of the print newspaper.

Of course Wenger doesn't claim he had perfect foresight. Like many people who encountered the internet (or the web) in its early days, with hindsight he feels he was too optimistic: the ability to publish online himself without someone else's approval or intervention made him see the internet as a democratising force – something he is now ambivalent about.

'That was the first thing: "Oh my God, anybody can publish." I basically created my own little inky-dinky MIT page two days later because I was like, "This is so cool." I, like many other people at the time, was caught up in this idea that because any-body could publish, it would completely transform everything. That was correct at one level. I was correct about really putting a dent into the businesses that were built on being gatekeepers to publishing. That is, music publishers, book publishers, et cetera – news publishers, in particular. No longer did I have to write a letter to the editor that the editor might edit and might not print, I could just put a rant somewhere on the internet. The thing that I don't think I or any of the other early people who were enthusiastic about what this might portend were antici-pating was that there was going to be a re-centralising force.'

Neither Wenger nor Borthwick tries to argue against the internet's role in concentrating power – and to an extent money – in the hands of a few big players. The combination of factors that each sets out is initially subtle, but builds to some-thing which starts to sound like a catastrophe for those concerned with protecting democratic power and accountability – a near-perfect storm of factors acting in concert.

'It's always hard to disentangle cause and effect, but the way I see it is more there were structural opportunities to build very large businesses that captured a lot of value and there was money to go finance those,' Wenger explains. 'This is a world that's awash in capital. So whenever somebody can build a very fast-growing business, he or she can finance that business ...

I think it has more to do with fundamental regulatory issues that we need to grapple with and that we haven't grappled with very well. It's those regulatory issues that have resulted in the possibility of building these very large networks and of exploiting a lot of the market power that has been derived from those networks and hence building these crazy returns.'

One factor both men begin with is an initially counter-intuitive one: because the protocols upon which the internet and the World Wide Web rely are designed to be lightweight and minimal, they don't track us online. HTTP, the protocol that transmits web pages across the internet, doesn't store any data on users – and so can't store information like shopping baskets, identity or similar.

These all got built on in different ways by individual websites later, through innovations like 'cookies', small text files placed on your computer by virtually every website you visit. The site can then check for a cookie next time you visit, and remember what you looked at last time, whether you're logged in and more. These cookies can track us across the internet if sites give, say, an advertising network permission to put a cookie on your computer. Despite HTTP having been built not to store any data on users, tracking has become the business model of the web, largely thanks to cookies.

Through the creation of large databases tied to those cookies, tracking on the internet is controlled by private companies, instead of a public body or by the users themselves. This means that our credit card details are held mainly by one or two companies we trust, so we go to them – whether that's PayPal, or Amazon, for example – and our identity is held by, say, Google or Facebook and so we use those to prove our identity elsewhere.

'My theory, and maybe I just keep reverting back to the identity and the payment stuff, is that these are two key linchpins because we didn't solve them,' says Borthwick. 'We solved them in a centralised way. Amazon's my credit card and Facebook's my identity. And now a man happily walks through the open internet with those two things and it's like – how are you going to do anything? Every time you've got to pay, you've got to go to the Amazon store, and every time you want to go and talk to somebody about who you really are, you need to go to the Facebook store. I just think those two things became critical to it, but I don't think it needed to be that way.'

Wenger takes this further: it's these databases that have become the primary force to centralise power and control (and thus also money) in the online world.

'At some level, you can think of all the big internet giants as just being big databases,' he says. 'Amazon is a big database of credit cards, SKUs [product lines] and purchase histories. Facebook is a big database of people's identity, their friend relationships and their status updates. Google is a big database of search queries, query histories and retrieval results, and web pages. Three of the big web giants that we think of are databases. Your account balance, my account balance is being maintained in a database.'

For Wenger the database insight is a particularly exciting one because he is a believer in blockchain, a relatively new technology best known for being what powers Bitcoin and similar cryptocurrencies – but at its core is a distributed database technology over which no one party theoretically has control. To its advocates, this could disrupt the online data oligopoly – but to its critics it's a convoluted and unproven technology with many side effects.

'The re-centralising force for the internet was these databases,' says Wenger. 'These databases are extraordinarily powerful and valuable because I as the maintainer of the database am the only one who sees everything and everybody else just sees a tiny sliver of it. I can run all these analyses that nobody else can run. They give me great power … One thing is, they've turned out not to be great stewards of that power. They clearly did not take their Spider-Man "with great power comes great responsibility" to heart.' He concludes: 'This is why it's a particularly interesting moment in time to revisit how the internet is organised because the maintainers of big databases have proven to be less than having the best interest of the customer in mind.'

In other words, he hopes the potential for blockchains to allow databases to be widely distributed, impossible to alter and publicly verifiable, could lead to a change in the power structure of the internet, which hands control to the companies sitting on the most data.

This matters because control over databases is even more important than it first appears, he explains, partly because of one of the most discussed phenomena of the online world: network effects.

These are most typically discussed, obviously enough, in the context of social networks, as it's here that their benefits are most immediately apparent. Let's imagine two social networks which have both been operating in one country for around a year or so. One has about 100,000 users, while the other has close to a million.

If you're a new user looking to sign up to a network, and you try both out, you're far likelier to find people you already know on the second network – and so also much more likely to get an invitation to join that one too. This means in turn that you're not only more likely to join that network, but also more likely to send invitations to others to join it too.

On that level – of having people we know in one easy place to send group messages, chat to each other and organise events – it is better to have one social network like Facebook, with 2 billion users, than to have twenty rival networks with 100 million people apiece on each. Unless such networks had means to inter-operate – and why would they, if they're rivals? – that could easily be much worse for users.

In practice, though, network effects go much further than just social networks, and gather power for whoever controls the networks. A pre-internet idea of a network effect can be found in, for example, railways: add an extra stop to an existing railway line, and it helps existing customers, who now have an additional place they can visit, as well as the ones living by the new stop.

'A network effect is, as you add nodes, which could be railway stops or customers, you create more value for everybody in the system,' Wenger says. 'I believe that network effects are one of the defining aspects of the digital age.'

These effects are everywhere, he says, because data is 'super-modular': on any given type of data, there are diminishing marginal returns. If I want to sell adverts to you, knowing your country is useful. Your city might be better, but by the time I'm getting your postcode too, it's not adding much.

Similarly, knowing your rough age is helpful, your age to the nearest year more so, your exact date of birth not so much. The key effect that makes for a 'super-modular' function is that knowing a little bit more about each separate thing has much more value – knowing your rough income, your rough location, your gender and your rough age, all together is worth far more than knowing just one or even two of those.

Wenger is essentially saying that in an era of AI, algorithms and machine learning, joined-up data points across a lot of areas have strong network effects, generating much more information and value than used to be the case. This means network effects go far, far beyond social media.

'The reason I'm saying all of this is because I think when people think of network effects, they often think about it too literally, like in the Twitter-type way. Like I connect with you, the

Facebook-type way. Even the internet, or railroad network. But there is a much more profound way in which network effects are deeply baked into the fabric of any production function that's based on data.'

The result of these data oligopolies, Wenger explains, is that a large majority of us – in the developed world at least – carry around supercomputers capable of speaking to any other supercomputer on the planet, and then reduce them into dumb terminals for big tech.

'An iPhone is a complete supercomputer,' he says. 'If you just go back like forty years, no amount of money in the world could have bought this much computer power – it just didn't exist …Then the second you fire up an app icon, whether that's Facebook, Twitter, Amazon, what have you, that supercomputer basically works only on behalf of that entity, and not really on behalf of you. You are reduced now to using your thumbs and the wetware between your ears, and you're holding a supercomputer in your hand, a supercomputer that can talk to any other supercomputer in the world.'

It's this situation – and our willingness as citizens and consumers to put up with it – that concentrates online power, Wenger says. And so long as that's tolerated, people will try to make money from it.

'That has made these monopolies quite as powerful as they are, because they operate millions of servers and we literally operate our thumbs. It's just such an asymmetry. I think that as long as we don't fix this asymmetry, we're going to keep creating opportunities for somebody to create very, very large monopoly-like businesses, and somebody's going to go finance those businesses.'

THERE COMES A time for any company that gets big enough when it suddenly realises things are much more serious than they used to be. Borthwick, an industry veteran, can remember that moment for AOL (America OnLine) – the internet provider of the dial-up era, still famous among a certain online generation for its 'You Have Email' tone (especially iconic in the UK, where it was voiced by national treasure Joanna Lumley).

AOL had sold its internet provision in the US as an unlimited online service – only to have constant service outages and disconnections, leading to its being sued by multiple attorney generals. This, understandably, caused a lot of panic in the company's boardroom – but also a lot of confusion.

'In the boardroom, the discussions at the end of the long, long meetings would basically be a bunch of individuals turning round to say "Why the fuck is this happening? Our service is just a toy," ' Borthwick recalls. 'Because AOL's roots came from gaming, we thought about the software as being just ... We hadn't realised it had become a utility.'

Borthwick believes that even years on from that reaction to backlash from AOL – when the web was much younger – founders are still hit by that kind of disbelief when it's suggested their service has massive negative consequences.

'When Zuckerberg thought post-2016 elections that it was a crazy idea that Facebook could have affected the election, that's what I heard,' he says. Someone in the boardroom recalled later Zuckerberg saying, ' "It's just my Facebook, where we were just poking each other. It's a crazy idea." '

That incredulity is alarming enough in the US context – a country that in theory at least has democratic and judicial institutions strong enough to investigate and act against electoral interference or misinformation. But Facebook is in many countries becoming synonymous with the internet – through its roll-out of internet with free access to its services in developing countries – even as evidence grows of WhatsApp and Facebook being used to spread misinformation and influence elections across the globe.

'I do think that the VCs, all of us, need to recognise that we are no longer playing with little toys and this is the whole world we are talking about and this is people's lives,' Borthwick notes, recalling being approached by a not-for-profit which seeks to improve internet access across the developing world. 'I think that they were looking for friends, advice or money and I said to them, "I can't support you, guys," and they were like what? And I was like this: "Your mission today, as I hear it, is to propagate internet access in several countries and if I look at the Third World countries that have had massive penetration of internet access in the last three to five years, somewhere between 60 per cent and 100 per cent of that access is Facebook." So it's basically to introduce Facebook into Myanmar, or into Nigeria … And I said, "I can't support that." They were like, "No, it's an open web." I'm like, "It's Facebook." '

TO MY SURPRISE, the online investors willing to spend time with me on the record had – it seemed to me at least – confirmed many of my worst fears and worst suspicions about the internet.

Yes, the decisions all sorts of actors made have served to concentrate power in a handful of companies. Yes, the data oligopolies are real, and if anything, more significant than I had previously understood. And yes, the system had served to make insiders who had the money to invest far richer than they were before.

The VCs I spoke to clearly saw themselves as different – people trying to do what they could within the system to avert disaster, or at least improve the system from within. But by this point they were clear-eyed on the internet as it really is, rather than the romantic internet of which we used to speak.

When asked about what might come next, though, their answers diverged. Wenger looked ahead – and saw danger.

'I do think we are very much at this fork in the road where you can easily draw a lot of dystopian scenarios that we might be headed for,' he said. 'We might very much be headed for as I call it the "us versus them state", where the state has built a big surveillance system that's not democratically controlled, that doesn't have checks and balances, that doesn't have an independent judiciary, et cetera. And that's coming down ... people are pushing up against it, we keep stretching the income and wealth distribution further. It's very easy to think of dystopian scenarios.'

Borthwick, on the other hand, set out his views on the dangers of our future by talking about our past. Shortly after agreeing that venture capital and the people behind it are seriously under-scrutinised, Borthwick said he would need to go off on a tangent – and started speaking about the First World War.

He began by talking about the introduction to Barbara Tuchman's book on the war, *The Guns of August*, which he'd been reading recently after hearing Bob Woodward talk about it in relation to the Trump White House.

'She opens up the book and she talks about in 1910 the King of England died,' he recalls (it is more likely he is thinking of the coronation of King George in 1911, rather than his predecessor's funeral).[15] 'All of the monarchs of Europe came to London and you had seventy monarchs and the eleven, or twelve core monarchs of Europe all walking down towards Buckingham Palace together arm in arm. And people were like "there will never be war again". And a few years later, the First World War started.'

The 'sheer insanity' of the period, the 'scale of death and destruction' that took place a century before had grabbed him, despite the horror of the subject matter, leading him down a rabbit hole of books, podcasts and more. Until then, 'I didn't know shit about the First World War,' he admitted.

'The whole world really just descended to the brink of complete chaos and so our ability to actually ... It really made me question at a fundamental level, the reasoned ability of human beings. You asked, couldn't a bit of adult supervision have helped? Well, if somebody had said, it's just Franz, the Archduke Ferdinand, nobody liked him anyway, then maybe ... But the Serbians ... it's just like there's always been a problem. We don't have to light the fire that ignites the world because of this, but insanity can ... so that's one thing.'

Second, Borthwick continues, was the way the complex network of alliances between the Great Powers of Europe dragged first the continent and then the world into a war few truly wanted. 'I think in the same way we have interdependencies now, data interdependencies that pull us together or just destroy us in ways we can't imagine.'

And finally – naturally – Borthwick thinks about what technology meant for the war. It certainly didn't slow the killing, he notes.

'It was fundamentally about technology shift, so you have these incredible scenes of tens of thousands of people on fucking horses with white gloves and their swords out ready to charge into machine guns. And the irony is the other side is also people on horses charging into their machine guns, and nobody's waking the fuck up to say, "They have machine guns, we have machine guns. Maybe we shouldn't be riding horses into that shit?" After two, three years, they did. It was just like you saw this incredible technology transfer happen in terms of the military, in terms of munitions, in terms of the invention of tanks, U-boats. These were like things from outer space. Nobody could imagine them. Technology drove a lot of the insanity. The last thing I'll say about it, I did say it was a rabbit hole, and I do think that we are today actually at war. I think that we have a low-grade information warfare that's taking place among corporations, individuals and governments ... I think that the most debilitating forms of war to come will probably be through the network, because that'll completely debilitate our entire society and the entire home front, to get the war front, because that's the way you can shut a country down.'

He is not quite done.

'This is why I want you to publish sooner rather than later, because I do think that we still have agency to actually do something about some of this stuff. I do. Maybe.'

No pressure, then.

5

The Ad Men

IT'S A GOOD rule of thumb in journalism – if not in life itself – to get very worried when people tell you something is so complicated that you shouldn't worry about it. Through the 1990s and early to mid-2000s, the financial sector told the world not to worry as it developed ever more sophisticated products, leveraging and connecting the world's debt.

Yes, they argued, it's complex – but it's been worked out intricately by people far cleverer than you, and in reality these complex financial relationships make us all safer. Too late we learned – after the new collateralised debt obligations and dozens of other elaborate financial instruments had failed – that we should have paid attention after all.

Complexity and technical detail are often used to try to stop us looking too closely, and they're used all the time when we try to think about the online world. There's nothing like a few seconds of acronym soup or technical jargon to make most of us zone out, and the language of the online advertising industry – which mixes technical jargon, financial jargon and endless ad-industry acronyms – is almost engineered to make us zone out.

Another red-alert warning sign is when people in a particular industry don't want to use their own product – and if any sector in the world manages to thoroughly tick all of those boxes, it's online advertising.

'The reality is, on my own personal computer, I use an ad blocker – and I'm not embarrassed about that.'

Brian O'Kelley's admission – that he, like hundreds of millions of internet users, uses software to block online adverts – initially doesn't seem like much.

And it wouldn't be, except for who he is and where he's speaking from. O'Kelley, a handsome man, well over six foot with greying hair, is sitting in a small meeting room named 'Peter Parker' – all the meeting rooms are named after superheroes – in the New York offices of a large advertising technology company.

He's wearing jeans, a grey hoodie and a T-shirt bearing the company's logo, AppNexus – which is only fitting, given he's the company's co-founder and has been its CEO for more than a decade, since founding it in 2007. His company has just been sold for an undisclosed sum, reported to be in the region of $1.6 billion (as shown in the last chapter, sales like this are known in the industry as an 'exit'),[1] to the telecoms giant AT&T, one of the world's largest internet service providers. And O'Kelley when we speak is on his way out, officially moving from CEO into an 'advisory role'.

His departure is more than that of a typical executive making his exit after his company is sold on, because O'Kelley has a good claim to be the man who invented internet advertising as we know it now. The advertising model O'Kelley created was replicated and perfected by others, and now forms the central business model of most of the internet. With his company sold, he's getting ready to leave that world behind, at least in part – and he's reflecting on the surreal experience he's had.

'It's really strange,' he says. 'It's strange to see people writing books about it. Princeton has a class in their operations research group on this auction theory. There's tens of thousands of people that work in this industry, billions of dollars of exits. It's very odd to be like "Yes, I came up with all this craziness", just a couple blocks over from here … And now I'm kinda retiring from it all.'

The industry O'Kelley is leaving is huge, and its reach and influence goes further still. You might think of Google as a search engine company, or as an email provider, or as the owner of YouTube, itself an online video giant. In reality, all of those services exist as a means to attract users to Google's real business: advertising.

In the last three months of 2018 alone – not the whole of the year – Google's parent company Alphabet made $39.3 billion in revenues, and $32.6 billion of that came entirely from advertising.[2] Everything else is just giving you a reason to look at the adverts, and to give Google a way of knowing which adverts to target at you.

This is even more stark at Facebook, which makes its money not just by showing you adverts while you're on its social network, but by giving advertisers information about you as you browse the rest of the internet, so they can better follow you around other websites to deliver ads. Facebook had revenues of $16.9 billion in the last three months of 2018 – and $16.6 billion of this came from advertising.[3]

Even Amazon, better known as an online shop – and by those in the business as a supplier of online servers, storage and services – gets billions in revenue from its little-known but fast-growing advertising business, taking close to $3.4 billion in the last months of 2018.[4]

These are some of the companies taking the biggest bucks, but the influence of the advertising model goes far further. We all know that advertising is the model that fuels the traditional online media, its new digital upstarts and even the new generation of YouTube and Instagram influencers.

But advertising also fuels a huge behind-the-scenes set of industries – most obviously, like its offline counterparts, an army of middlemen designing, tracking and placing adverts. The vast ad industry is also the catalyst for the new wave of data companies, looking at tracking our behaviour ever more closely and ever more pervasively – occasionally to the advantage of hackers, when they get their hands on it, and frequently to the advantage of government agencies addicted to data in the online era.

KNOWING THAT WE are constantly tracked as we browse has become a matter of dull, background acceptance for many of us – it's inescapable, hard to understand and mainly just annoying.

Anyone browsing in the EU is now all but conditioned to unthinkingly click a pop-up that appears on every site asking them to consent to the use of 'cookies and other technologies' to 'customize your experience, perform analytics and deliver personalized advertising on our sites, apps and newsletters and across the Internet', usually alongside a lot of other small print.[5] That quick, unthinking, click of 'yes' doesn't just allow targeted adverts on the site that offers it, but allows it and the advertising networks it works with to follow you around the internet. And most of us click 'yes' dozens of times every day.

A quick visit to nytimes.com will load up twenty-one different trackers, a catch-all term for snippets of code designed to follow the user around the internet and monitor how they're consuming content (and where they've been). You can look up what trackers are used by different sites yourself by downloading a browser add-on called 'Ghostery', which can both identify and block such trackers.

Nine of the nytimes.com trackers – 'Amazon associates', 'BlueKai', 'Google AdWords Conversion', 'DoubleClick Floodlight', 'Twitter advertising', 'Facebook custom audience', 'Google Publisher Tags', 'Yahoo DOT tag' and 'Snapchat For Business' – are marked as directly relating to advertising. A trip to CNN loads twenty-eight trackers, fifteen of them advertising. Thesun.co.uk loads up thirty-five, including fourteen ad trackers. And the tech site wired.com fired up no fewer than forty-four trackers, eighteen of them advertising.[6] The number of trackers on each site varies depending on how many ad networks they work with, how much data they collect and how their own site is built.

Even just the little bit of the picture we can see as end users shows we are being tracked on an industrial scale – but that's not the half of it, as Brian O'Kelley can explain. He has good reason to know, as it's all – at least in part – his fault.

Online advertising is notoriously complex, but if you're just looking at the core concepts – rather than trying to work out if you're paying the right amount for your ad campaign – it can be much simpler than is usually admitted. It's also more worrying than they'd ever let on, but it's making a lot of people rich.

'I think there are a handful of people who understand it, like really could understand and explain every single link in that chain, but for me that's from fifteen years of building the entire thing,' says Brian O'Kelley.

Here, then, is the inside story – the jargon-lite version – of how the multi-billion-dollar industry that built Facebook, Google and others evolved, and what that's meant for the rest of us.

It starts straightforwardly enough, as the early days of online advertising was fairly simple: websites wanting to run banner adverts, or ads at the side of their content, would pick an ad network to manage their advertising for them. They would then receive a certain amount of money for each thousand people (this is known across the industry as a 'CPM', which stands for 'cost per mille') who saw the adverts – often, in those days, guaranteed by the advertising networks.

In theory, if you were the owner of a blog, or a news website, you faced a fairly simple choice: pick the best ad network for you which will make you the most revenue. If one network was offering a $3 CPM and another was offering $1, the choice would seem a no-brainer.

The reality was quite different: rival advertising networks would define a 'view', or what kind of view they would count, in very different ways that would be almost impossible to work out in advance by the owners of a website. So a network which seemed to offer a great rate might only accept one in ten of your site's visitors as an actual viewer – dramatically lowering your actual rate. This is where O'Kelley stepped in, creating what is now known as 'programmatic advertising', which has come to be the main way ads are shown on the internet, though it began life as a simple tracking tool.

'It was sort of an accident that I created it, I didn't mean to,' he recalls. 'I was working for a little start-up called Right Media, which was an ad network. My observation was that publishers, like people who had their own websites, would put ad networks on their page to make money, but were being really irrational about which ad network to use. There was one network called Fastclick, and they would say, "Well, we'll pay you $4 CPMs," which was incredibly high at that time.'

Fastclick, he explains, seemed to be offering ten times more per thousand ad views than its rival networks – an astonishingly good deal. The problem was it had much higher standards for what it would count as a 'view' than other networks. It would throw out anything that it couldn't be sure was exactly the kind of customer it was looking for – meaning that out of, say, one million actual visits to a site, it might only count 10,000 of them as 'real'.

This made the task for publishers all but impossible: how could you work out which ad network would actually make you more money, given they all defined views differently and the supposed headline figure of CPM was useless?

O'Kelley's idea was to try to build a quick dashboard tool to help publishers track which ad network would actually make them more money, once you factored in all of their requirements.

'I built a yield management widget, basically, that would try to figure out which ad network to allocate to, based on which would make the most money. But it didn't work, because the ad networks were too dumb.'

In other words, the ad networks weren't sure what yield they could expect to get off a particular advert either, as they weren't very good at tracking their own revenue. So O'Kelley's independent widget for publishers became part of a wider system: his company sold better software to ad networks to help them track how much a given advert would yield.

If this is starting to sound a bit like a price comparison site in reverse – or even an auction – then that's because that's exactly what it had become. And it had begun, O'Kelley insists, with the best of intentions for publishers.

'It basically became programmatic advertising where, in the blink of an eye, the publisher holds an auction across all the different advertisers, and then the highest bidder wins. It was built on this idea of helping publishers make more money.'

It took off quickly – so quickly that O'Kelley's then boss was keen to sell the company and cash out. Right Media was bought out by Yahoo in 2007 for $850 million, of which O'Kelley says he only saw a relatively small share.

'I had a huge fight with my boss, he was the CEO and I was the CTO [chief technology officer]. He was like, "We're selling this thing," because it was a rocket ship. I was like, "You're crazy. This is going to change the world." We were both right. He fired me and sold the company.'

TO UNDERSTAND PROGRAMMATIC advertising, it might help to jump back and look at what happens behind the scenes when you get ready to click on a website which serves online ads. This is the jargon-heavy bit – but we're going to motor through it at speed to try to keep it simple and digestible.

The detail, though, is telling. Before you've clicked on anything, it's likely an advertiser somewhere has decided they want someone like you. The whole point of programmatic advertising is a kind of matchmaking game: it wants to match you, an internet user, with the brand that is most keen to show you their advert – and therefore the company that would pay more than anyone else to get in front of your eyes.[7]

Typically, that brand will start with a list of its recent customers, or people who have signed up to its mailing list. The brand wants to target people who are similar to those recent customers – in age, gender, social class and income, or other factors. They hand that data over to a data management platform (DMP), which may then get in touch with a data broker – companies which buy up data on us from dozens or hundreds of sources – to 'enrich' the data, for example matching up postal areas to data on average income, to see which type of person on the list is likely to be richer, and so worth targeting.

A sample of this enriched data is then sent to a demand side platform (DSP), whose role is to find people similar to the ones on the list it's just been sent – and then show them adverts at the right price. That platform will have these ideal audiences in mind for possible adverts for hundreds, or thousands, of brands – and there are hundreds, or thousands, of these platforms.

The next step of this process relies on you: if anyone's going to show you an online advert, you need to be browsing the internet. When you click to visit a site, it starts doing what it needs to in order to show you the content you want to see – its editorial content – but also sends a request for adverts to a supply side platform (SSP), which it instructs to get in touch with you directly. That SSP then asks your browser for all the information it can get from your cookies, plus details of your browser, your IP address and more.

We now have a DSP with data on the type of user it would like, and an SSP with at least some data describing what sort of user (you!) is visiting a website it provides the adverts for. The two are now matched by ad exchanges, which send on the data from the SSP to dozens or hundreds of DSPs – what used to be ad networks – each of which checks the ads they have in stock for the one that best matches what they know about the user, and comes back with an offer of how much they'd pay for that ad slot. The winner's advert is then what you see.

As a typical internet user, when you first hear about this process, it can sound ridiculous. Yes, we know that when we browse the internet, the site we visit learns a bit about us, and the three to four advertisers we see on the page probably pick up a bit too. We might not be thrilled about that, but given we're getting something for nothing, that feels fair.

The previous paragraph suggests something different entirely: in the fractions of a second between hitting a link and waiting for the page to load, it suggests your data is sent out to hundreds, then thousands of places, who then each seek to match it against sets of data – some of which almost certainly also relate to you – and a bunch of algorithmic guesses about you, and then each places a value on your head.

That would mean every single click sends your data cascading to thousands of places across the internet, each of whom can try to build up their profiles based on it. It seems impossible, everything seems to happen too fast – but that's exactly what does happen.

O'Kelley strips out the technical details and explains it in sixty seconds like this:

'In some ways, it's like the actual technical details aren't the point. The point is that, for me at least, your cookie is sent out to maybe a hundred, maybe more, different firms, and they say, "How much will you pay to buy this ad spot for this cookie right now?" They are then merging that with any historical data they know about you that they've purchased from various vendors, maybe trying to merge it with other browsers or devices you have, maybe your offline postal address, doing anything they can to match it with something that tells them more about you. Then they're going to match that to advertisers they've sold deal to, or pass it on to another Right Media ad network. All this is happening, in this blink of an eye, between when the website loads and the ad loads.

'What's really happening is this crazy auction of your personal information to almost everyone on the internet, such that the highest bidder, arguably not the highest bidder, wins. What's more important to me is that all the losers still know you visited that website. You say, "Well, they just know my cookie." No, there's an entire industry that's trying to match your cookie to all kinds of information.'

This last point is particularly important: if we want to track what's happening to our data, or take control of how we browse the internet, we need to have some visibility over what's happening. Lots of places seem to base their logic on this being possible, but in practice almost everything that gets done with our data happens completely behind the scenes – perhaps on the other side of the world – and can be done with only basic information, like cookies, travelling to and from our own browser.

In 2018, with the General Data Protection Regulation (GDPR), the EU made the most ambitious, and complex, data protection rules in the world – with massive penalties of up to 4 per cent of global revenue facing companies which engage in serious malpractice with their customers' data.

The problem, O'Kelley says, is trying to work out what's happening in the first place – the system is so complicated, and so much happens out of sight, that bringing it to light is all but impossible. One thing we can know is that there is a huge problem, and maybe a huge breach of law: a core principle of processing data under GDPR is informed consent. But how can consent be informed if we have no idea what's actually happening?

'Even in the industry, I don't think people really understand it very well,' O'Kelley explains. 'When I talk to publishers, advertisers, agencies, even people who work at ad tech companies who should know better, there's a lot of gaps. We create all these acronyms, the DSP, the SSP, and all these things. I'm like, "Yes, I was there when we created the acronyms," and they don't mean what you think they mean. They're very handy, acronyms, but they don't mean anything. If you want to confuse someone, say "Oh, that's the SSP". It's like any made-up term, it means something different to you than it means to me. I have the luxury of having built these systems, of seeing it from day one.'

The result of seeing it from the beginning, he says, is seeing that the companies that are trying to monitor what gets tracked online by looking at the browser – because that's the only bit we as users can see, and so our only starting point to work out what's happening – are essentially doomed to miss the real story.

'A good example of this is GDPR, which is itself so freaking complex that no one understands it ... there's entire companies formed around GDPR. They're like, "Well, we're going to see every cookie that browser drops, and that way we're going to know what happens to private information,"' he says, exasperated. 'It's like, "Guys, 80 per cent, 90 per cent of the data transfers is server-side, it never touches the browser." That's like saying, "I know where all the ice is, because of the icebergs that tip out at the top." It's 100 per cent not right.'

This problem becomes easier to think about when you consider what's happening on your computer with cookies versus what's happening behind the scenes. A cookie itself is a tiny file – an entry in a database – on your computer, just logging basic details like when you last visited a page. But my computer at the time of writing has 2,934 of these cookies on it, and lots of them come from the same companies. Once I visit a site, the company operating it can log on its own computer as much as it likes about the behaviour connected to the cookie it saw – how long did it stay on the site, what did it look at, and so on. Others can track which cookies are seen alongside each other, to identify me by patchwork.

Companies can buy up, trade, share and sell the data, but I as a user can't ever build up that picture, even with laws that are supposed to protect me behind the scenes. This is what O'Kelley means when he talks about an iceberg – but it's not clear we're even seeing the tip of it.

The Cambridge Analytica scandal – where the political consultancy was found to have bought up data on 87 million people via an online personality quiz – brought down the company and brought huge public fury. The story was important and the company was rightly criticised, but the scale of its data was trivial compared with the scale of the really big players.

In fact, Cambridge Analytica's data was almost useless to them, given the sheer scale and power of the advertising and targeting tools Facebook itself (and its rivals) holds.

Not only does this model of using much more of our data behind the scenes than is apparent to us up front mean that we're being watched, tracked and targeted to a much higher degree than we can fully know, it's also another driver of the internet concentrating power and creating monopolies.

An internet populated by thousands of small advertising networks – each working in different ways – might offer a greater diversity of business models, of intervention, and would in theory mean that publishers, the people who actually create what we want to read, listen to and watch, get a decent share of the proceeds. But when everything is data-driven, the advantages go to whoever has the biggest scale, and so the richest data. That can mean the data brokers – companies like the credit reference agencies, who no longer just keep information relevant to your credit score, but also buy up and track data from hundreds of other sources about you, which they then in turn sell on – grow in power, but it rewards companies like Google and Facebook too.

Given it sold for a reported $1.6 billion, it may seem a ridiculous statement, but O'Kelley's company AppNexus is a relative minnow in the online ad world – one of the biggest 'independent' ad tech companies (at least until its sale), but tiny compared to the real giants.

Part of that is because once someone has come up with something like programmatic advertising, it's easy to copy. O'Kelley even employed the man who he says copied his ideas on programmatic advertising when he worked for a rival firm, DoubleClick, which was then bought by Google.

'Michael Rubenstein, who is our president, was at DoubleClick at the time – he was responsible for their ad-exchange efforts,' says O'Kelley, laughing. 'If you put in your book that he copied me, I'd appreciate it ... he'll just laugh. Because it was his job to copy it. It was literally his job.'

Before buying DoubleClick, Google had an ad model – which it still uses in part – that was much less invasive. Instead of trying to guess who you are using data and so show you adverts that match the demographics of a brand's customers, Google could do something much simpler: show you adverts based on what you were searching for. It doesn't take any invasive personal data to know, for example, that someone searching for 'budget holiday Magaluf' is someone worth targeting a cheap holiday ad at.

By adding DoubleClick to its repertoire, Google managed to extend its advertising dominance just in time, now being one of the biggest ad networks displaying ads across the internet, not just on its own sites.

Given Google also created Chrome (a web browser – the software used to access the web, such as Internet Explorer or Firefox), Android (a mobile phone operating system) and more, its data pool keeps widening, and its advantage grows and grows – and regulators seem to just tinker at the margins, with even apparently huge and dramatic legislation like GDPR seeming to make almost no difference in the day-to-day business model of the ad-funded internet.

'The reality is governments are terrified of the internet,' O'Kelley says. 'I think part of my frustration is that, at least in my little world of advertising, self-regulation wasn't good enough because Google had too much power … To their credit, they were actually one of the better actors on the internet, but they were impossible to compete with because they had too much monopoly. They owned a fucking browser! I can't compete with that. I do think it's bad for competition. I think it's bad for users. I think it's bad for a lot of things that Google has aggregated so much power and that governments have let them continue to aggregate and not held them accountable.'

THE NEXT CONSEQUENCE of the data-driven ad model that O'Kelley laid out to me came as a shock – though perhaps it shouldn't have. Programmatic advertising was built to help publishers, but has done the exact opposite. O'Kelley places a large part of the blame for that on those publishers themselves. The way it's doing the damage, though, isn't at all the one that most of us think about.

And the consequence of the way the whole thing works isn't just responsible for quality journalism getting less revenue, it's also directly responsible for the thousands and thousands of junk websites, delivering weird slideshows like 'Young Jenny

From *Forrest Gump* is 34 Now and Gorgeous',[8] 'Stars Who Show Almost No Gratitude or Class',[9] 'Celine Dion's Many Tragic Struggles Revealed',[10] or '56 celebrities you didn't know are gay, bisexual or lesbian'.[11]

These are the junk food of the internet: taking the list of 56 celebrities as an example, the content is just old trivia rewritten from Wikipedia and others news sites – without credit, of course – and then split into an article which only shows two celebrities at a time. To read the full list requires you to click twenty-eight times, reloading the adverts accompanying the article every time. Once, that kind of trashy content would attract such low advertising rates that it wouldn't be worth making – who would want their brand next to that stuff? – but things have changed, making companies like Outbrain and Taboola, who specialise in this and are known as 'content farms', hugely lucrative.

It's considered a truism in the news industry that the internet is killing journalism. The standard rationale is that first newspapers lost classified adverts (ads for jobs, homes for sale, used cars, etc.), which used to be one of their biggest earners, because once the internet came along – with its searchable forums for such ads – it was just simply better than what came before. This was followed up by more and more people giving up buying their daily paper, in exchange for news they could get for free online, and then online adverts paying far less than print adverts did.

That's all true as far as it goes, but there's a special problem with programmatic adverts that seemingly none of the publishing industry has woken up to. Roughly speaking, it works like this: in the old era of print advertising, a brand would pay more to advertise in the *New York Times* than in a free newspaper handed out at shopping malls.

There are a number of reasons for this. In small part, brands pay for the prestige of being attached to the *NYT* brand, but really they're more interested in the fact that the average *NYT* reader is wealthier, better educated and far more likely to be in a good profession than the typical American. In addition, someone who pays for a subscription to a newspaper is far more likely to actually read it than someone who's just handed a free paper on the way to their car.

In the online era, advertisers are just as keen to reach the kind of people who read the *New York Times* – or the *Guardian*, the *Washington Post*, the *New Yorker*, the *Atlantic*, *The Times* or any one of dozens of premium publications – as they ever were. In theory, they should still be able to command a hefty amount more for their advertising than the junk content that surrounds them. But in practice that premium is much smaller than it could be.

The reason? They're happily telling advertisers who their readers are, and those advertisers can then go and target those readers elsewhere, for much less cost. News outlets are giving ad networks the means to go elsewhere to advertise to their readers – and don't even seem to notice they're doing it.

By participating in the data-driven ad world, publishers are hastening their own demise.

We saw earlier that when you visit nytimes.com, nine different advertising networks' trackers pick up that you've made that visit. They can even see how often you visit the site, and how long you stay there, if they so wish. That means those nine networks – who operate adverts across the internet – now know that you're a regular *New York Times* reader.

If they have clients who want to target regular *NYT* readers, they now don't need to actually pay the *NYT* for one of its ad slots. They can instead keep following you around the internet and wait until you visit somewhere cheaper – perhaps after catching up with your quality daily for the news you read a junk list or two (we all do it), and now ad networks can catch you there instead.

Once you're flagged as being a high-value advertising target – by one or more ad networks being aware of this thanks to the cookies on your machine – the content the ad is being displayed next to becomes almost irrelevant.

Because via cookies any junk news site can know I'm a *New York Times* reader, or recently shopped at a high-end store, or similar, O'Kelley explains, ad networks like Facebook and Google can put high-end adverts next to low-quality sites. Unlike the old world where the quality of the content matters, now it's all about the cookie.

'Facebook benefits the most from this because they can send crap traffic to websites all around the world, like "Oh, this is a high-value cookie", or buyer, even though this is clearly crap content.'

The result is a chain reaction that the quality news brands often see themselves as being a victim of, but are in fact fuelling by opting-in to the broken advertising model of the internet, where tracking is seen as intrinsic and inescapable. If the *NYT*, for example, didn't offer ad trackers on its site, the only reliable place for an advertiser to target their readers would be their own website. By O'Kelley's reasoning, they're part of why they're losing ad revenue.

'It's about the systems that build the internet. It's the dopamine, grabby headline,' he says. 'I don't know if it's an instinctual thing, but I'm reading an article, a good article, and at the bottom there's "17 shocking photographs from airports", and this very attractive woman leaning over her luggage. I'm like, "Goddamn it, they got me," like, "Why am I reading this shitty headline on this terrible thing?" It's going to take me to seventeen different pages of screenshots of attractive women, and at the end I'm like, "I want more." It's almost like a slot machine. Everyone's going to make a whole bunch of money, except it's like cotton-candy money. By the time I'm done with that, I'm not anywhere near that website. I've contributed a huge amount of money back into this crappy ecosystem, and continued the basic *Avenue Q* thesis – that the internet is for porn.'[12]

As O'Kelley notes, in that situation the quality content provider has got the adverts from one page view, while the content farms making the junk have got dozens, all the while knowing they have a high-value user, too.

'It's a huge sucking sound of money going away from the *New York Times*, going away from the *Guardian*, toward effectively Facebook and this Facebook ecosystem of random sites. Taboola and Outbrain are another example of this, where every time you click on those links at the bottom of an article, you're leaving the quality content and you get into this crazy world of intent-driven content farms. Content farms are killing us.'

IF IT'S SO much against their interests, why would almost all of the world's major publishers voluntarily participate in the world of online targeted adverts, given no one is forcing them to? Most seem to believe that they have no choice: their business model relies at least in part on advertising, and it is taken as a truism that targeted adverts raise more revenue than dumb ones. Given that companies are worried about losses, and many have revenue targets and shareholders to satisfy, they can't afford to leave money on the table.

That's the logic – but it's rarely been tested. Until now.

Alessandro Acquisti is professor of information technology and public policy at Carnegie Mellon University in Pittsburgh, and much of his research focuses on what he describes as the behavioural economics of privacy. Most recently, that work has looked at just how much extra revenue the privacy-invading targeted adverts that pervade the internet actually raise.

It turns out to be a question with two very different answers for the networks that distribute the ads – the tech giants – and the publishers who make the content.

Acquisti's research is aimed at testing a core claim of the internet: that we as consumers and citizens benefit greatly from having a huge range of content and services available to us for free, and tracking and targeting are essential in order to be able to provide those.

'In the last few years, I started noticing that more and more entities, especially from the advertising industry, were making claims about the benefits the consumers gain from the collection of their data,' he explains. 'Claims that were not necessarily false, but were – and I find it quite interesting – not necessarily empirically vetted yet. Such as, for instance, the claim that increasing data collection, collecting more data and more granular data is in fact critical to the provision of free content and free services online. This claim is extremely widespread, and is, of course, originating from the advertising industry but also in the world of policymakers as well as researchers. What's interesting to me is that it is a very plausible and legitimate claim – until you start trying to dissect it and try to look at the evidence supporting it.'

What Acquisti realised was that there had been almost no efforts to find an actual causal relationship between the boom in online tracking and the boom in online advertising spend – both had very clearly happened, but no one was in fact looking at the actual effect of running targeted versus non-targeted adverts. So he and his research team built a complex model using data from 'a large American media conglomerate' which aimed to control for other factors (audience size, demographics, etc.) and look at the actual effect on its revenues of running targeted adverts. The results are shocking.[13]

'We found that the increase in revenues received by the publisher for ads which are targeted was at most 8 per cent. It was certainly a statistically significant difference and it was also economically significant – 8 per cent is better than 0 per cent increase in revenues, but it's a little surprising when you consider that merchants who pay for ads tend to have to pay much more than 8 per cent to target their ad.'

This research suggests that the benefit to the publisher for running targeted adverts could, in practice, be tiny: for every $1,000,000 it takes in advertising revenue, using this ad model could gain it an extra $80,000 – as Acquisti says, not nothing, but a very small compensation given what we know the detrimental effects are of publishers giving away their audience data to the ad networks.

But what about the other side of the deal? Behind all the middlemen – the DSPs, SSPs, ad exchanges, DMPs, data brokers and quite probably a traditional ad agency or two – lies the brand that wanted to run the advertising campaign in the first place. If running a targeted advertising campaign is only worth 8 per cent in extra revenue to the publisher, how much more does it cost the advertiser?

Acquisti and his colleagues are still trying to work this answer out, as it is fiendishly complex to analyse from the outside. However, he does have some research using a different methodology – he is keen to make clear the two are not directly comparable, but only give us an impression of what's going on – looking at how much extra brands pay for targeted campaigns.

'We see scenarios where the targeted ads cost 500 per cent to the merchant relative to the untargeted ads,' he reveals. 'Basically, five times more. Five times more. Now, this sounds an astronomically large differential relative to what the publisher ends up getting.'

This is not the definitive figure, and we should treat it with the caution Acquisti tells us to – but it nevertheless tells us something very strange is going on. Brands are being charged five times as much for well-targeted ads as they would be for a general campaign, but by the time you get to actual publishers, they only see a relatively small increase in their revenues. This at least hints that someone in the middle is getting very rich – perhaps unfairly.

For Acquisti, the research so far raises deep questions for the advertising industry, and whether the multi-billion-dollar global behemoth – dominated by the tech giants – offers anything like the benefits it claims, and whether it's anywhere close to being as essential as it's supposed to be.

'I'm really interested to see how true the claims are,' he says. 'Whether most of the money ends up going to the middleman or whether, in fact, most of the money goes back to consumers in terms of free content – these are important issues.'

Acquisti notes that the internet had done perfectly well at delivering free content – and supporting it with advertising – before the world of endlessly targeted adverts existed.

'The free resources and free content on the internet already existed way back, twenty years ago,' he says. 'Advertising existed already at the time, but it was not targeted. Then, Google arrived and started doing contextual targeting. Initially, it was not behavioural targeting. It was contextual. For instance, if I see, in an email, that you are talking about cats, maybe I show you an ad for cat food. If I see that you're searching for a vacation, maybe I show you an ad for vacations. That's contextual. What happened? ... Basically, after 2004, meaning after Facebook entered the game, because Facebook was a game changer, we started adding more and more ability to cross-link internet users' behaviours across different sites. It's related to the ability to recognise the consumer coming to, for instance, a news site as the same consumer who before had got excited about cat food and before had gone to a site about vacations.

'Therefore, we started getting this ability to target ads.'

THIS STARTS TO explain the apparent complexity of online advertising – it helps the companies in the middle make the profits that they do.

'You know what? At the end of the day, publishers and marketers have to stand up for what they want,' O'Kelley says. 'Marketers want good advertising on good sites, publishers want good advertising on good sites. It's the middle. Everybody else is finding ways to screw everybody.'

Sometimes that's just a matter of using the complexity of the ad market to make a much bigger margin than might otherwise be possible. Sometimes it's a question of using market power to command a huge price premium for your sales, knowing that there are very few other places for companies to go. Sometimes it's a question of a company's chief financial officer and chief marketing officer knowing they can load cost onto the marketing budget and it will work out well in tax terms, meaning they don't need to look too closely.

But sometimes it's outright fraud.

An article by Max Read in *New York* magazine,[14] posted at the end of 2018, gathered together and summarised work on online advertising, audience metrics, advertising metrics and more, finding that huge swathes of the key statistics of the internet were at best shaky and at worst entirely fake.

Clicking through the article – after first dismissing a pop-up asking 'Can we continue to tailor ads for you?'[15] – detailed offence after offence in the online world. Some ad networks were using automated web browsers, or 'bots', to mimic human traffic and drive up ad views with fake clicks. Then it moved on to broader problems: listing scandal after scandal in supposedly reliable online metrics tracking audience numbers or video views, examining the world of fake followers and fake subscribers, and automated content mills scraping other sites for cheap traffic.

Fraud, fakery and bogus content, it seemed to argue, was just how the internet is – a culture and a need built up over years, with people seeking every trick at their disposal to pick up their own share of the apparent wealth on offer.

If the online ad world has got so far away from what it was supposed to be – and if almost no one we might want it to benefit is getting the returns – what does O'Kelley, who considers himself an ethical ad man, think we can do to fix it?

Perhaps unsurprisingly, he doesn't think we need to give up on adverts – he believes that it's perfectly possible to make lots of money from online ads without being creepy. As an example, he says it's often the case that just using time of day and which site someone is on is enough to have a great idea of which advert to serve them.

The first step, he says, is for publishers to realise they are taking part in their own downfall.

'Publishers are promiscuous. They will work with anybody. Anybody who offers them money they say yes to, and then they complain they're getting screwed. I'm like, "People who take money from anybody that offers it to them and then claims that they're getting screwed ... there's a term for that."'

Moving on – for publishers at least – means calling an end to letting the ad networks take data on your audience. In other words, on us – ad networks, after all, can't get these details on us if publishers don't hand them over.

'Have some standards. Get into meaningful long-term high-value relationships with advertisers and you'll get what you should get,' is O'Kelley's advice to publishers. 'Turn over your ads space to anybody who wants it. How many companies out there just profiling and watching people who happened to go through, say, the *Guardian*, and then using that to go find them on cheaper sites? Hundreds? You can't really complain. It's not like they're tapping into the wires, you are giving them this inventory, you are doing it to yourself, stop complaining.'

O'Kelley acknowledges this is tricky when in at least the short- and medium-term this tactic could temporarily hit publishers' already strained revenue, and acknowledges that specific legislation – like GDPR, but tougher – could help without requiring such drastic action from publishers.

'I want to know, any time my cookie is being marched to something else, anywhere,' he says. 'I don't think that's too much to ask. I don't think that's going to break anybody's business model. It's what I expect. I think GDPR, with a couple of tweaks, could be really good. As written, it's just too obtuse to make it actually do that.'

Overall, though, O'Kelley thinks the era of personal ads should end – and that it could, if we had the will to do it.

'I'm pretty cynical about the way that advertising works right now. It's so close to being good. Just get rid of the personal data part, and all of a sudden, this is actually a really efficient eco-system. What'd be really smart then is to look at the attribution side of who purchases, which you don't need any personal information for. All the algorithm needs to know is which ads influence that purchase. We can do all of this without sharing personal information. Micro-targeting, individual targeting, behavioural targeting – I'm just pretty convinced that the incremental value of the micro-targeting, versus the societal and overall internet impact, is nowhere worth it. By moving that dial one notch back, you shift $1 billion into the hands of quality journalism and advertisers. It works better.'

Of course, all of that is easy to say and exceptionally hard to do. But how does the world as it is now look to someone who's been at the top of the industry for nearly two decades, and has one of the strongest claims to have pushed it in the direction it's ended up? The internet is home to the world's biggest businesses – and many of those businesses are ad giants.

'I would just say that we think about who controls the internet, I really care about where the money goes – watching the money flow,' O'Kelley says. 'You go to a website … you go to another website and it all starts again. Every step you take it just repeats again and again and again. The money just keeps aggregating and aggregating. It's just when you really think about your financial footprints on the internet ... at the end Google takes a piece of every single click on the internet. It's amazing. It's an awesome process. Think about all the internet users. All the ad buyers. All the ad tech companies. All the data vendors. All the ad agencies. All these different people that are just profiting from whatever you do. They all get a little piece of everything. It's pretty interesting, to me at least. It's just the sheer number of people who profit.'

I point out to O'Kelley that his reflection comes from the position of having cashed out from one dotcom sale in the mid-2000s, and now just months before selling AppNexus for more than a billion dollars. There are, I suggest, worse vantage points from which to look back – surely that money colours his legacy?

'I feel like it's a Pandora's box problem,' he finally concludes. 'In there somewhere there's hope, like I did have hope that this was going to actually make things better. I think it did make some things better, but along with hope came all these other evils. It's hard to see enough good and enough progress to make it worth all the other crap that came with it ... I fought that chaos and that sort of negative consequence for fifteen years and in many ways I lost. If you say I selfishly made a lot of money and made a lot of my employees money and their families money but we didn't make the world a better place ... I don't feel great about that.'

Part Three
THE MELEE

6

The Cyber Warriors

IT WAS A June night in 2013, and I was one of two people watching a progress bar crawl – painstakingly slowly – towards 100 per cent. We were on the fourth floor of the *Guardian*'s London offices, two storeys away from the newsroom, in a 'secret project' view well out of everyone's way. The room is usually used for projects senior management want to keep away from reporters – desk moves or possible redesigns. But this time it was something quite different.

Almost everyone else in the building had gone home hours before, leaving, unwittingly, just me and David Leigh – who until just weeks before had been the newspaper's investigations editor, and who had already been dragged out of retirement – sitting in near silence watching a progress bar advance around 1 per cent every five minutes, missing out on a balmy summer's evening.

The reason we were sitting there was that we were confident it would be worth the wait, because if everything worked okay – and that felt like a big 'if' – we would, just as soon as that progress bar hit 100 per cent, become the first UK reporters to set eyes on thousands of documents revealing the activities of GCHQ, the UK's signals intelligence agency.

That progress bar was tracking the decryption of tens of thousands of top-secret intelligence documents leaked by the NSA whistleblower Edward Snowden. Not even he had read them all, but from his time working with the USA's intelligence agency, he'd relayed one tip of what to look for, and this was

143

all that we'd have to go on as a start. We had no details, no explanations, no lengthy guide. We had a note with one word on it: 'TEMPORA'.

We had no idea what it was, or what it meant, but for investigative journalists, like any other gossip, there is no greater bait than a hint at a mystery, especially one that apparently is on the verge of being solved.

Shortly before midnight, the bar finally hit 100 per cent and we had the ability to search a hugely classified database explaining what the US and UK government surveillance agencies really did. We leaned into the computer and typed in 'Tempora'. A few dozen documents appeared, mostly complex and technical, documents that would clearly take days or weeks to make sense of.

One of the documents among that batch, though, stood out: a slideshow summarising a visit by General Keith Alexander – then the man who oversaw the National Security Agency – to Menwith Hill, a US intelligence base situated in otherwise sleepy Yorkshire countryside.

'Why can't we collect all the signals, all the time?' it reported the head of the US spy agency saying. 'Sounds like a good summer project for Menwith!'[1]

THE DOCUMENTS EDWARD Snowden provided to the *Guardian* and the *Washington Post* came to shed unprecedented light on how the USA had come to exploit the internet which it had helped build – not just for intelligence, but for a form of online war too. The internet might feel like a private and safe space. The reality is anything but – as we came to find out over the summer months of 2013.

The story had begun a few weeks earlier, on the other side of the Atlantic.[2] Janine Gibson, then the editor of *Guardian US* – the outlet's effort to build a largely stand-alone online offer to break the USA – was called by Glenn Greenwald, employed by *Guardian US* as a comment writer on civil liberties.

Greenwald excitedly set out an outlandish situation to Gibson. He'd been contacted by an anonymous source through an encrypted email. Not knowing what to do with encrypted email, he'd ignored it – but the source had reached out to someone else he knew, who'd read it, and got in touch. The source was claiming to be a whistleblower with top-secret material disclosing mass surveillance by the US government. He wanted to meet in person and hand it over. And Greenwald thought he was for real.

At around this point, Gibson suggested they probably shouldn't be having that conversation over the phone.

Gibson found herself having to make a huge number of decisions, almost all at once. On the one hand, she might have one of the biggest national security scoops of a generation in her lap – but on the other, she might also be on the verge of spending thousands of dollars of newsroom resource on a fantasist, or a deliberate hoaxer. Even if real, she could face a huge backlash from the US government – if she published something false, those repercussions could be much worse.

She opted to follow the story. Greenwald was sent to Hong Kong, where his as yet unknown source had made elaborate plans to meet: he would wait in a hotel foyer with a Rubik's cube, and they would follow him without saying hello from there. But because Greenwald, while a hugely popular blogger and an experienced civil rights lawyer, had never worked as a news reporter, she insisted he be accompanied by the *Guardian US*'s veteran Washington DC editor Ewen MacAskill. Her newly hired security editor Spencer Ackerman would bolster the team working from New York.

And to round the team out, on a trial basis at least,[3] I was invited along for the ride. Gibson arranged for me to fly over from London, as I was a reporter whose speciality was data and document leaks, having worked for WikiLeaks before joining the *Guardian*.

The details of what happened next fill several books, documentaries and even a feature film. But at its crux it began with the decision by Gibson – aided by her deputy Stuart Millar – to launch the first story on 5 June, revealing a domestic warrant by a secret US court to Verizon, allowing the collection of data on millions of US citizens. Earlier in the day the deputy directors of every federal agency had pressured Gibson and Millar not to run the story.

Unable to believe the final decision could possibly lie with Gibson, US officials sought her boss Alan Rusbridger – who was uncontactable on a flight to New York to work on the story, but who had fully delegated all key decisions to Gibson in the meantime. Having failed to get him they then even roused their colleagues in MI5 to wake UK-based *Guardian* staff to see if any could overrule Gibson. None could.

The story ran and immediately led bulletin after bulletin. And then the next day came another, then another – and then that Sunday, Edward Snowden revealed himself to the world in a video interview with Greenwald, MacAskill and film-maker Laura Poitras.

Given he had worked for them, Snowden knew the meaning and contents of what he handed over on the USA's intelligence agencies. But he had suspected the UK's agencies would be doing much the same, so had taken classified internal documents (routinely shared with the US) from the UK's GCHQ (short for Government Communications Headquarters) signals intelligence agency which he handed over to MacAskill in Hong Kong, before destroying everything still in his possession and attempting to flee to Ecuador – only to get stuck in Moscow, where he still resides. It was these documents, this untouched cache, that had found its way to the *Guardian*'s London offices.

GENERAL KEITH ALEXANDER had been the head of the NSA (National Security Agency) for eight years at the time the Snowden revelations surfaced, and had been an enthusiastic advocate for expanding the agency's role in the post-9/11 expansive surveillance environment.

Bulk surveillance had always been a far more contentious topic in the USA than in the UK, thanks to a much less comfortable approach towards government and legal precedents in favour of privacy. But in the online era, with such huge volumes of data flowing into and through the USA, agencies were keen to get their hands on as much as possible, so as never again to miss an attack so badly as when they had failed to prevent the horrors of 11 September 2001.

The job of head of the NSA was always the role at the very edge of these civil liberties issues. The CIA was required by its mandate to focus on overseas citizens, and worked through human intelligence. The FBI was primarily a law-enforcement agency. But the NSA's speciality was signals intelligence – something that once meant tapping phone lines, monitoring satellite communications and tracking radio signals.

In the twenty-first century, it mostly meant something else: tracking the internet – and in that US-dominated network of networks, where people from across the world would use US companies, US servers and US cables to communicate. In the old days, it would have been entirely legal for the NSA to monitor a telephone call of interest between someone in Iran and someone in Syria – so why should it suddenly become different if they're now both using Gmail and its US servers, or Skype, and so US networks? Developing the USA's online capabilities while staying on the right side of the Constitution was maybe the thorniest problem in US intelligence.

Alexander (whose PR representatives declined an interview for this book) was widely seen as being on one side of that debate: collect it all, expand it all, and worry about the legal niceties when the time came for analysts to look at the material that was collected. A profile in *Foreign Policy*[4] depicts an evangelist for the mass-surveillance approach, keen to give tours of his Star Trek-style command centre, replete with a 'Captain Kirk' chair, banks of monitors and even sliding doors that would 'whoosh' as people entered.[5] For a man in charge of such vast and intrusive surveillance powers, he was viewed even by his colleagues and predecessor, the report claimed, as a 'cowboy'.

The NSA's capabilities didn't just stand by themselves, though. Alexander's role made him the most powerful partner in the modern world's most impressive spying alliance: Five Eyes. This coalition is at its strongest between the signals intelligence agencies of the five countries who take part. They have bases in one another's countries, share staff, and share each other's access points to the world's satellite networks – and to the internet.

Almost everything that any of those five countries – the USA, the UK, Canada, Australia and New Zealand – find is automatically shared, whether new information, new techniques or new sources.

And so while the USA's mass-surveillance capabilities increased vastly under Alexander, it wasn't there that his vision was best realised – it was in the UK, under an experimental programme. Its code name? Tempora.

The Tempora programme serves as an illustration of what happens when a government has access to some of the key interchanges of the global internet, a strong relationship with the telecoms company that runs them, and the budget and expertise to build a sophisticated surveillance operation.

At its most basic, the idea of Tempora is this:[6] intelligence agencies could easily have a need to access someone's call history, or messaging history, or recent browsing, at short notice. At its most dramatic, imagine they get a credible tip-off that someone they've previously never heard of might be on their way to commit a terror attack.

What they would really want in that situation is to be able to see their recent communications, to see if they discussed an attack and where it might be. But if they'd never heard of that person before, being able to do that would rely on having kept – for a short while at least – that information on pretty much everyone.

That's what Tempora set out to do – essentially acting like a catch-up TV service (like Sky+ or iPlayer) for the whole internet. We know that data traverses the internet in packets, travelling across the world as bursts of light down fibre-optic cables, many of which travel through the UK, the US or both.

Using something as simple as a glass prism, that light can be split – creating a perfect copy of all the data travelling along that fibre-optic cable for GCHQ to collect and analyse as it sees fit. And thanks to their friendly relationships with the telecoms and cable companies, both the US and UK governments have come to arrangements to get this kind of access.

Most data that travels down the cables is, by volume, streaming video from YouTube, Netflix and similar services. By throwing this out and keeping only the plaintext that they could see, GCHQ could build up a trove of data of the traffic going into, out of or through the UK. Given the vast volume of information concerned – and to try to stay compliant with human rights laws – the content of communications collected this way is kept for three days, and the metadata (who sent it, who to, IP addresses, location and similar information) is kept for up to thirty.

Data collection on this extraordinary scale was justified by a rationale that the government had done nothing to invade anyone's privacy until an actual human being dipped in and took a look at your messages, browsing or other content. The fact of it being collected – or even of it being analysed by algorithms – is, so far as the UK's legal approach is concerned, no problem whatsoever.

Even in agencies used to seeing vast amounts of intelligence and huge volumes of data, Tempora was something special. Not for nothing was the Tempora programme part of a wider programme at the agency known as 'Mastering the Internet'. Enthusiasm for the programme had infused the whole GCHQ agency: at the end of a top-secret presentation offering legal training to analysts being briefed into gaining access to the programme came a cheery note:

You are in an enviable position – have fun and make the most of it.

As citizens of the online world, we've got so used to the idea of people watching us – Google, Facebook, Amazon, advertisers and perhaps our governments too – that it's often hard to feel any real reaction to the revelation of something like Tempora, and in the UK at least the response to its revelation was muted.

Part of that is because most of us, probably rightly, figure that we're never going to come up on the radar of the intelligence agencies, and since we won't … what of it? In reality, the existence of that data opens its potential for abuse by a future government uncommitted to our democratic norms, or simply to abuse by an employee – spying on their ex-spouse, for example. Algorithms misfire and subject people to arrest, surveillance or harassment.

But there's also a creepy factor that's just missing from the online world, as it feels less real than the offline one. If we learned that the government was intercepting every letter we sent and received, making a photocopy and sending it on, we might be perturbed. If we then learn they're also tapping our phone calls, monitoring our text messages, bugging our house and monitoring our bank card, we might start to freak out – even if nothing else happened. Learning they threw it out every few days wouldn't be a huge comfort. This is, of course, exactly what's happening to people whose online data traverses the UK – British people and millions of others around the world whose data crosses our networks – but because the online world feels less real, it somehow doesn't cause alarm.

The British comedian John Oliver tried a blunter approach when he interviewed Edward Snowden via videolink from an undisclosed location near Moscow on his HBO show in 2015. Oliver showed Snowden clips of Americans being asked about surveillance – and Snowden himself – on the streets of Manhattan, and shrugging with indifference.[7]

Then the interviewer asked the people on the street a slightly different question: should the NSA be allowed to keep people's nude photos? Interviewee after interviewee indignantly said any programme that allowed the government to store or view such pics would be an invasion of privacy, should be shut down, and would be a sign things had gone too far.

'The good news is there's no programme *named* "the dick pic programme",' Snowden noted, bemused, after being shown the clips.

What he knew, though, was that there was no shortage of naked photos in the databanks of the NSA and GCHQ. Part of this is just a jump of logic that we can often miss: if the government is, temporarily at least, storing almost everything that it can from the cables, then any adult content that gets sent will be caught in that dragnet too.

But things go a little further than that: Snowden, as a former employee of the US intelligence agencies and their contractors, spoke of a culture of passing images around. Documents verify his case – and also suggest that for GCHQ, at least, the huge collection of adult imagery it had accidentally amassed was becoming something of a problem.

In 2008 GCHQ set up a programme it code-named Optic Nerve,[8] which collected imagery from Yahoo webcams making video calls to one another. The agency found it technically simpler to just take and store still images every few minutes from every camera rather than to try to target its surveillance on the webcams, and so did that on more than 1.8 million users over a single six-month period.

The issue GCHQ appeared not to have considered was that many people used webcams to share explicit content with each other – the agency estimated about 7 per cent of content saved through the programme was some form of adult image, meaning the UK spy service had apparently by accident amassed one of the world's largest pornography collections.

Policy documents suggest some staff, at least, may have forgotten to treat such material professionally. 'You are reminded that under GCHQ's offensive material policy,' one document sternly notes, 'the dissemination of offensive material is a disciplinary offence.'

The 'dick pic programme' might have been a little more real than even Edward Snowden realised.

THE INTERNET EXPANDED the possibilities for signals intelligence agencies such as the NSA and GCHQ in ways that were never before imagined, making it practical for the first time to collect information on entire populations in close to real time. The open question has been whether the tens of billions of dollars spent to make this happen was money well spent – and intelligence chiefs like General Alexander have done little to make that case.

Defending one particular NSA mass-collection programme to Congress in the wake of the Snowden revelations, Alexander said collections of this type had helped foil more than fifty terror plots, leading to headlines across the globe[9] echoing his comments and appearing to justify his strategic approach. Bulk collection might make a few civil-liberties types uncomfortable, but who can argue with foiled terror plots?

It turns out the not-for-profit US newsroom ProPublica could.[10] They asked Alexander and the US intelligence agencies for evidence to back up the comments to Congress, and initially faced a diminishing count of plots foiled that could be directly attributable to the programmes Alexander had cited.

ProPublica persisted, and eventually the NSA declassified details of just one plot that this approach had thwarted: a man in San Diego who had sent $8,500 to Al Shabab, a militant group in Somalia. The NSA has a longer, classified, list of plots sent to Congress, but has offered no more justification than a single sub-$10,000 bank transfer foiled as public evidence for a multi-billion-dollar programme.

Internal assessments of Alexander's approach – and the bulk collection approach that has seen Five Eyes agencies become obsessed with the internet over human intelligence – could be even more withering. In his *Foreign Policy* profile, officials who had worked with Alexander described his habit of showing off impressive-looking network diagrams, of who had contacted who, turned into huge charts with phone numbers with dozens of connections coming off them at their centre. Those nodes, apparently, would be at the centre of the network.

One officer claimed to have looked into those numbers after one such meeting: they weren't terror network masterminds. They were the local pizza restaurants.

THE MODERN-DAY DESIRE for Western governments to exploit their online advantage shows that the relationship between the US defence establishment (and its allies) and the global network it was instrumental in creating has only got more complicated as the internet has grown in power and significance.

On one level, the internet is a great tool of soft power – it can function as a symbol of free speech and communication, of entrepreneurship and of a globalised world. Such an approach relies on encouraging countries across the world, even those who are not traditional US allies, to embrace the internet.

That instinct is opposed by a desire to exploit the advantage the internet brings in more direct ways: if you have dominance over the internet – which will now indisputably be the engine of the post-industrial era – why not exploit it directly, and use it for intelligence and military advantage?

Revelations of the activities of the US, UK and their allies have already served to neutralise the idealistic power of the internet: by routinely spying on their own populations, as well as those of their allies and adversaries, they have given those who would use the internet even more malevolently the excuses they need.

Regimes around the world have proven the internet does not need to come as a package deal with increasing freedom: China's 'Great Firewall' effectively limits any political messaging the government does not want its citizens to see, and the country's rulers have no difficulty tracing those who would defy its restrictions. In Syria, the Assad regime used the mobile networks and internet – and Western-made spying software – to track down and arrest or kill its opponents. Examples abound across the globe.

If this were all just a case of information gathering – a digital game of spy versus spy – this would be dramatic enough. But the internet of today is far larger than that: for one, most major corporations are connected to it, making them ideal targets for hacking attacks aimed at stealing intellectual property, bidding information and more – something the Chinese state is often accused by Western governments of carrying out on a massive scale as part of its bid to create its own high-tech economy.[11] Businesses are caught up in the intergovernmental conflict, which means normal people are. Want to get into a corporation? The easiest way is to hack one of its employees.

The potential for government conflict across the internet to affect us as regular users goes even further, though: today lots of industrial machinery is connected, directly or indirectly, to the internet. So too are power plants, dams, train signalling systems and other key bits of our infrastructure. Hacking doesn't just let an attacker see how these are being used: it can let the attacker take control of those systems themselves – and break them.

This was most dramatically unleashed in 2010, in an attack against Iran. Inside their nuclear-enrichment sites – where uranium was being enriched to weapons-grade quality – cylinders on the site began behaving erratically, spinning back and forth rapidly in a particular and deeply destructive pattern. After a short time behaving in this inexplicable way, the cylinders would explode, damaging the site and disrupting the country's nuclear programme.

The cause of the explosions was eventually found – by Symantec, a US-based cyber-security company – to be an extremely sophisticated form of cyber attack (a 'worm'), which targeted the exact model of industrial controller software used in Iran's plants. The worm had been made so aggressively, though, that it accidentally spread to millions of computers, thankfully doing no damage – though had the payload (the part of the worm designed to do damage) had similar errors to those that made it spread too aggressively, the outcome could have been disastrous.

The architects of the attack were eventually revealed to have been none other than the NSA, working with Israeli intelligence, and receiving some support from UK intelligence. With no declaration of war – which would be required for such destructive action using soldiers, or a bomb – the countries had caused physical damage in an adversary nation. The laws of armed combat do not apply online – and so far as we can see, it's the Western powers who have fired the first shot.[12]

Making this murky world still murkier is that the agencies in charge of mounting these kinds of audacious attacks are often the same agencies in charge of using the internet as a surveillance tool. But they typically share a third duty too: they are also the agencies in charge of protecting their respective governments, businesses and citizens from attack, as if they weren't already conflicted enough.

GIVEN THE HIGH STAKES of the online game the world's spy agencies are playing, it's perhaps no surprise that in the summer of 2013, the patience of the UK government at least was rapidly fraying.

In the USA, the Snowden revelations had sparked a mass wave of public outrage, forced President Obama to make a public statement promising to review laws on mass surveillance, and received enthusiastic support and coverage across the US media. This, coupled with the USA's First Amendment protecting freedom of the press, meant reporting on the leaks could continue in earnest – though the same protections were not extended to Snowden himself, who fled overseas rather than face prosecution under the Espionage Act.

This was not the case in the UK. Though the surveillance revelations eventually led to a string of legal victories challenging the scope of mass surveillance,[13] much of the British press – who have traditionally enjoyed a friendly, even cosy, relationship with spy agencies – turned against the *Guardian* and its reporting.

The UK government had a weapon in its arsenal its US counterpart did not: it could threaten the newspaper with an injunction against publishing any more articles, with punishing – potentially business-ending – penalties if it did not comply, including in its US subsidiary. The government did not want the backlash for doing this, but did want the reporting – from the UK at least – to end. The *Guardian* would not willingly stop reporting, and certainly wouldn't hand over material, but could not ignore the injunction threat.

A farcical compromise was hit upon. The UK government was aware that the *Guardian* had a backup of its GCHQ cache located outside the UK, but accepted an offer from the newspaper to destroy all copies of all material on UK soil – provided the government would promise not to seek an injunction. Overseen by two unsmiling GCHQ staffers, three senior *Guardian* editors smashed, buzz-sawed and magnetically erased about £10,000-worth of computers and hard drives, even as journalists relocated to the USA to keep on working. The NSA reporting had continued to be done from Janine Gibson's *Guardian* US office – and now the GCHQ reporting was done from there, too.

The development, with hindsight, was a very lucky one – because the next article being reported caused bigger flare-ups with the agencies on both sides of the Atlantic than any other, and became the only story the NSA flat-out asked the newspapers reporting it not to run. We didn't understand why at the time, but the story laid bare the choice the agencies had faced: do their best to protect their citizens online, or keep their surveillance advantage.

It showed they had openly and knowingly chosen the latter.

What was puzzling is that when we first embarked on it, the article hadn't seemed so much more controversial than what had gone before. The story wasn't about Iraq or Afghanistan, secret informants or sources – we never published anything like that. To us, it seemed less contentious than our revealing that the NSA had celebrated in a congratulatory memo spying on thirty-five friendly world leaders' phones.[14] It was a story about online encryption. How controversial could it be?

Encryption, it turns out, is one of those things that sounds either boring or unintelligible to about 95 per cent of us, but which lies at the core of huge and genuinely important disagreements when it comes to computing.

The key to the importance of encryption is understanding a way in which the online and offline worlds are profoundly different. Offline, if I buy or invent an armour-piercing bullet, it only benefits me. And similarly, it's possible for me to go out and buy new, better armour, and give it only to my own troops. The two decisions are totally separate, and only really affect me (or my country).

Online, things work differently. In this world, most forms of attacking a system rely on you knowing about a way to get in that whoever is running the system doesn't intend – the equivalent of a door left unlocked, or a window with a broken latch.

Imagine you discover a new vulnerability in, for example, Apple's iOS software that runs on its iPhones and iPads, which you could use to gain access to any iPhone in the world and spy on its owner. This is akin to learning that hundreds of millions of homes across the world – many belonging to people on your side – have an unlatched window. Either you can tell no one, and exploit the vulnerability you've found for your own advantage, or you can tell everyone – and the latch will be fixed.

If you choose the first option, though, someone else might find that vulnerability too – in fact, they may have found it long before you did. And so from that point, any attack – whether minor or catastrophic – is one you could have prevented. This is a constant dilemma for intelligence agencies, given their dual role being in charge of arranging defence against attacks, while also being in charge of intelligence gathering. They have a direct conflict of interest.

This is a broad issue for the agencies in the online world, but gets even more serious when it comes to encryption. Without some form of encryption, any message that your computer sends and receives over the internet can be read anywhere it travels through, whether that's your internet provider, a random server on the way, a government, or someone else. If information is stored unencrypted on, say, an online store's servers and they get hacked, all that customer information (your address, password, card details and more) has been exposed.

Strong encryption, then, is everyone's only bet against having their personal details leaked or hacked – but also thwarts the intelligence agencies, who without it have a much easier time accessing and searching everyone's communications in bulk, to find the needles they're seeking in an ever-expanding data haystack.

Encryption relies on being knowable by everyone: it's not a secret. When people come up with a new protocol for encryption, they announce it publicly in full, and then other experts try to see if it works – mainly by trying to break it. If it seems to hold up, that's evidence it's a strong enough standard to be worth using.

Given this is what protects our banking system, our critical infrastructure, our WhatsApp messages and more, this stuff matters.

All of this we learned over a few painstaking months as we worked to report what had been happening with the NSA, GCHQ and encryption – teaming up with ProPublica and the *New York Times* to give the story maximum impact. As such, it didn't come as a total surprise when both Gibson and Jill Abramson – then the *New York Times*'s executive editor – were asked by the NSA, for the only time in the whole Snowden reporting process, to kill the story entirely.

Both took just minutes to consider the requests. Both said no.[15]

The story, when it was published, confirmed the worst fears of all but the most paranoid security expert: in their most heavily classified documents, the NSA and GCHQ were boasting they had made 'vast amounts of encrypted internet data ...

exploitable', and had led an 'aggressive, multi-pronged effort to break widely used internet encryption technologies'.[16]

They had not only breached these through advanced maths or raw computing power, though – they had been spending $250 million a year to 'covertly influence' technology companies' product design to their own advantage, while at the same time GCHQ was also working to access encrypted data within Microsoft's Hotmail, Gmail, Yahoo and Facebook. This was roughly the equivalent of learning that the police knew about weaknesses in every door lock in the country, and had been secretly working to make the locks even worse.

Particularly unnerving were the code names given to the programmes by the two agencies. The NSA code-named its efforts against encryption 'Bullrun', after one of the earliest significant battles in the American Civil War. The UK's GCHQ did the same, naming its programme 'Edgehill', after an early conflict in England's Civil War. It's hard to imagine, given these names, that the agencies were unaware of the double-edged nature of their efforts.

The situation we are left with, then, is one where governments and their agencies failed to set up laws governing conflict on the internet even to match the relatively weak and minimal ones that exist in the real world. They set up agencies to defend us hobbled from the beginning with dire conflicts of interest that would compromise their mission. They attacked and undermined the very technologies that could serve to protect us from crime as well as from attack. Perhaps these decisions were inevitable, but the result is an internet which – even if we don't notice it – is anything but peaceful: every day, there is a constant, hidden conflict.

And we're the ones caught in the middle.

THE PROBLEM IS even more intense and immediate for big businesses, who make prime targets for criminal and nation-state hackers alike. A fairly typical sign of how seriously banks and similar companies are forced to take the issue can be found in the UK bank RBS's legally required disclosure of major risks to its business in its annual report.[17]

> The Group is experiencing continued cyberattacks ...with an emerging trend of attacks against the Group's supply chain. [C]yberattacks [are] increasing in terms of frequency, sophistication, impact and severity ... In 2018, the Group was subjected to a small but increasing number of Distributed Denial of Service ('DDOS') attacks, which are a pervasive and significant threat to the global financial services industry ...
>
> [T]here can be no assurances that ... measures will prevent all DDOS or other cyberattacks in the future.

The reality of life online is a complex set of battles between states, businesses, criminal hackers and regular internet users – with companies turning essentially to the online equivalent of mercenaries to defend their systems. One of those online defenders is Symantec, the company who discovered the Stuxnet worm targeted at Iran's nuclear-enrichment facilities.

Symantec is US-based but keeps facilities across the world, and works to protect clients there. Brands like Symantec and Kaspersky are familiar to regular users as our anti-virus software – if we've heard of them at all – but behind the scenes these companies work in a much more sophisticated way, operating war rooms to look out for major events and tackle them when they occur.

One of these 'secure operations centres' (SOCs) is located in Fairfax County, Virginia, on an industrial estate a few miles out from the nearest town. Getting in requires going through a high-tech man trap and staff's use of outside electronic devices is tracked.

Inside, teams of analysts track the clients the company is protecting, including hospitals, energy companies and infrastructure giants. Symantec's role is trying to protect its clients from attacks by criminal attackers and foreign governments, a role that in the real world would be left to law enforcement. But in the online world, with its mixed incentives, that doesn't seem to work – law enforcement is interested in securing convictions after an attack (difficult when hackers are so often overseas), while companies want to prevent the attack in the first place.

'When I used to work in the FBI we used to say we only catch the dumb criminals,' Steve Meckl, Symantec's director of Managed Security Services, says from the SOC's war room, which has a series of desks surrounded by giant screens showing the current status of the systems the team is monitoring. It's only partly for show. 'This is the room where we will all gather during crisis activities if we need to have meetings between the teams,' Zack, one of the senior analysts working for Meckl, notes. 'It's also the place where we give our SOC tours. We've got all these big screens, why not use them?'

Meckl – who oversees one of Symantec's three cyber-defence teams – was not criticising the FBI, where he spent a decade of his life, but instead setting out how law enforcement is almost systemically broken online.

'We're way, way better on the commercial side,' he says. 'It was astonishing when I came over to Symantec how much better we are at catching threats.'

The difference, Meckl explains, is that the private sector can voluntarily be given extensive access to the networks of their clients. The FBI and other public agencies are restricted by what they can obtain through warrants and legal authorities. 'The US laws are set up to make it difficult for the law enforcement to do their job because you want to protect people's rights, which is a good thing in my opinion.'

What necessitates the private sector getting involved is that companies like Symantec or its rivals can see much more, much earlier, than any law-enforcement agency.

When a company hires a firm to help with its cyber security, that company will typically install sensors (either software or actual physical devices) on its networking equipment, servers and computers – monitoring in a great deal of data the activity of that router or machine. These can include checking for known viruses or worms, but also tracking how much data it is sending or receiving, scanning traffic passing through the machine, or any number of other sources of data.

The company knows this is being shared and monitored because that's what it's paying for, and so it also trusts it will be kept confidential. The result for Symantec is that every day its teams across the globe receive more than 151 billion logs from devices operated by its customers.

Those logs are then automatically analysed for material out of the usual, generating around 65,000 potential threats on a typical day, which will then be graded in order of severity and looked at by the company's analysts. A serious or critical threat, of which Symantec will see around 200 per day – for instance, a targeted attempt to hack the laptop of a client's CEO – will be prioritised and flagged to that company.

On most days, these threats are familiar and isolated. But sometimes things are different: a new critical threat appears in one client's system, and then another, and another, and another.

'If something like that pops up on one customer network, we immediately start looking for the signs of it across our global customer base,' Meckl says. 'This actually happened with WannaCry.'

If any one attack exemplifies the mess the cyber warriors have created – the consequences of the ongoing government versus government battles, agencies hiding their knowledge of vulnerabilities, and the ease with which an attack can spread, far beyond the control of its maker – it's the May 2017 attack that came to be known as 'WannaCry'.[18]

The attack also shows the bizarre world of responding to such threats – in which one security researcher working on his own proved more useful in staving off the threat than major intelligence agencies and security corporations.

For people in the UK, the first sign that something was wrong was reports from across the National Health Service that its computers were failing. Computers were locking up, and then restarting with a locked screen saying the system's contents had been encrypted – and would be kept locked unless a payment of $300 in Bitcoin (the anonymous online currency) was made within three days. After three days, the price would double. After seven, the data would be irretrievably deleted for ever.

This is a type of attack known as ransomware, named because it holds your computer and data hostage in hope of a quick profit if you pay up. But something about this attack was wrong: ransomware is best targeted at home users, who lack backups and easy access to IT support, and who need their data.

This attack, though, appeared targeted at major corporate networks – and it was spreading alarmingly fast, to targets with nothing in common. Within hours, dozens of NHS hospitals had been hit, as had Telefonica in Spain, and major networks in Russia, Ukraine, India and dozens of other countries.

The first step to dealing with WannaCry was working out what it was and how it was spreading. Who was behind it and what their motivation was could wait for later.

For companies like Symantec, something like WannaCry shows up via their log files – and probably through panicked calls from clients – and then escalates quickly.

'It was Mother's Day weekend and I was in Rowe, Massachusetts, with my then fifteen-year-old, for a hockey tournament,' says Jeff Greene, Symantec's head of global affairs. 'WannaCry started breaking and we contacted some folks we know. I know we talked to the UK government and the US government and said, "Hey, do you guys need any help?" The response was, "Oh my God, yes." That weekend was spent sharing malware samples.'

The short-term fix for WannaCry, though, didn't come from Symantec, or GCHQ, or the NSA. It came from Marcus Hutchins, a UK-based independent security researcher, who discovered the WannaCry attack in effect phoned home to a particular web address for instructions – but no one had actually bought that web address. On his own initiative, he bought the domain and had it serve as a kill switch, preventing the wild spread of the attack, for a time at least.

Over the following weeks and months, the truth of the WannaCry attack emerged. The reason the attack had spread so quickly was that it was based on a sophisticated attack the NSA had developed, which the agency had lost control of, and which had been posted online for virtually any hacker to find.

WannaCry was a destructive payload – which encrypted and destroyed all the data on affected computers – attached to the very effective means of distribution the NSA had created, a crude bashing together of two sophisticated attacks.

It was not, however, a means of securing ransoms: US intelligence eventually pinned the blame for the attack on North Korea, though they have little idea what its intended target was, or whether it was simply a bid to cause chaos. In that, at least, it succeeded: the damage to the UK's health service alone was estimated at £92 million. And because once code is online, it can be taken and tweaked by anyone, WannaCry or variants of it keep resurfacing, sometimes run by actual criminal gangs seeking ransoms, sometimes to cause chaos, sometimes with no obvious motivation.

'Not this weekend but the weekend right before that, I did what I would do on a normal Saturday,' recalls Zack, the senior analyst. 'But Sunday I spent twelve hours on the phone fixing a WannaCry outbreak. It's still happening.'

WannaCry was a very public example of the most embarrassing kind of intelligence agency misstep. A US government agency discovered a vulnerability in Windows, affecting millions of systems around the world. Instead of working with Microsoft to build a fix, it built a sophisticated attack using the vulnerability, which then got taken from it by rival hackers and posted online. It was then used as the basis for a global cyber attack, first by North Korea, and then by criminal gangs.

And as if determined to make the whole mess as ridiculous as could be, the US authorities added one final twist for the security researcher who found the kill switch: they arrested him, as he attempted to fly home from a conference in Las Vegas, just weeks after the first attack. Researching online security often means demonstrating vulnerabilities – and Hutchins claims it is precisely this for which he is now being targeted by the US government. More than eighteen months after his arrest, his case is still ongoing.[19]

The world of online hacking stopped being about hobbyists a long time ago: it's now a world of government versus government, of industrial espionage, and of seriously organised crime – if stealing your card details will make the most money, expect efforts to do that. If it's something else, they'll move on. And they'll exploit any new and innovative attack like WannaCry to do so.

'There are many signs that attackers have gone from the stereotypical somebody working out of their mom's basement,' Meckl says. 'These are criminal organisations that are constantly shifting their technical expertise and investments in different types of attacks because the profitability landscape shifts. When Bitcoin was really high, people worried a lot of coin miners' malware was going out there. They were leveraging your computer to mine cryptocurrency for themselves and taking their own energy costs out of the equation, so they can become profitable. Now that cryptocurrency seems to be crashing at the moment, people are shifting back to other types of attacks ... stealing passwords or credit cards.'

Jeff Greene reflects that the internet has ended up in a very strange place – though not necessarily one that's bad for his business. 'It would be great if we had to manufacture bad news or a mandate,' he muses, imagining a world where there were few enough real online threats that he would have to overhype them to get the attention of lawmakers, before noting that there's enough real trouble that no one would need to do so.

Greene, who used to work as an adviser on Capitol Hill, says that there's no good way to define what private companies should be doing to protect their users – versus what governments should be doing to protect their citizens – in the online world, as all the offline comparisons break down.

'The analogy would be, if the Germans, the Japanese had tried to bomb the factories in Detroit building the US armaments in World War II, it wouldn't have been left to Ford and General Motors to protect them ... But you do expect Ford and General Motors to have security to prevent someone from walking in and stealing their corporate IP [intellectual property]. It wouldn't be the US government's responsibility in World War II to make sure that they lock their safes at night to make sure that the plans for whatever tank they're building isn't stolen.'

The US government has had longer than any other to consider the relationship it would like to have with the internet, to model to the world. From its inception it has chosen to try to exploit the internet to its advantage, to seek an edge in maintaining surveillance capabilities, and often to prioritise the chance for cyber offence (or espionage) over defence.

It may come to regret those decisions as online power shifts, in a mirror to offline power. China is building its own technology sector, building sophisticated hardware and its own social networks – and buying up Western tech companies: in 2018 the Chinese gaming corporation Kunlun bought out the gay hook-up app Grindr,[20] while tech conglomerate Tencent took a stake in the long-standing social network Reddit in 2019.[21] The US might not have been quite so benevolent an overseer of the internet as it made out, but it kept to many norms that others may not uphold.

Recounting a conversation with a Chinese citizen working in the industry, Jeff Greene notes a clash of cultures. 'He's basically, "The US does the same thing everyone else does." I'm like, "No, we don't." He's like, "You spy." I'm like, "We spy all the time, but we don't engage in economic espionage."' Greene just couldn't see how the US could engage in intellectual property theft. If nothing else, if they stole the design for a Huawei router, how could they ever decide which company to give it to, and what would they do when the other sued?

'There is such a cultural disconnect between what is acceptable in China [and in the US]. When the Chinese are in trade negotiations, I'm sure we're trying to steal everything that might help the talks advance. When Exxon is in discussions with China drilling, I don't think that there's a US government entity trying to steal China drillings and give them to a new company.'

In other words, Western intelligence agencies see it as part of their job to obtain information that might help their economies as a whole, in a general way – by trying to see what another country's real red lines might be in trade talks, or what they'd concede. But they wouldn't try to hack a company in a rival trading nation to steal its intellectual property and pass it to a different private company. China does exactly this – but also seems to believe that everyone else does it too, no matter how much we deny it.

China taking spying further than the US would is hardly the only unintended consequence we could face, in terms of allowing the internet's potential for enhancing social control by government. India is trying to build a centralised database of its citizens' information, known as Aadhaar, which is raising serious civil liberties concerns.[22] China is introducing the concept of 'social credit', a variant of a credit score for your citizenship as monitored and defined by the party, a capability clearly reliant on the internet and its surveillance capabilities to work.[23] Examples abound, on great and small scales, across the planet. The US made the decision to exploit its dominance of the internet – it is not at all clear whether they considered what might happen if that dominance was not permanent.

If the internet was the twenty-first century's equivalent of the frontier, government decisions time and again appear to have favoured lawlessness and danger. This is perhaps because the internet went so rapidly from a closed community of US government staff and academic researchers, to a fringe community of nerds, to the bright shining hope of capitalism, to suddenly being critical infrastructure. And all of that happened with few of us paying attention and fewer still thinking even one step ahead.

But the government is not entirely responsible for why there are so many rich pools of data to obtain from the internet, for those who would seek them; perhaps part of why intelligence agencies have been so tempted to harvest data from the internet is because it generates so much of it.

As we've seen, the core of the internet's harvesting of data is its business model: the overwhelming majority of the open internet is funded on advertising. It is a truism among those who work in such companies – including Google and Facebook, who have taken a place among the world's largest by their approach – that online advertising relies on targeting, and targeting relies on knowing a lot about whoever is browsing. That's the very core of their business.

The result, as Greene observes, is a generation who have almost given up on privacy: if you feel like half the world is looking at your data already, who cares if the government's doing it too?

'I used to teach a class at University of Maryland Law School on law and policy. Before I did cyber, I prepared for that class, ready to go in. I remember thinking "They're going to be hardcore civil libertarians. Maybe there'll be a couple of outliers." I was going to be the "how many babies need to die before the government can read your public Facebook post?" type positioning. I got in there and they were all like, "The government reads all my emails anyway. I don't care." I had to do a complete 180. It was frightening both how wrong and how comfortable they were with it… I hope we've had a shift, but we have a generation that's grown up both assuming they don't have privacy and being okay with it. That's a really bad trend for the US and the rest of the world.'

This is the world that advertising capitalism has built, a world in which our expectations of any kind of private life are disappearing, and leaving us feeling disempowered against both our major corporations and our governments. Did anyone see this coming? Are free services in exchange for adverts worth the price we're paying, and the monopolies they generate? I had a lot of questions.

So I decided to talk to the people supposedly in charge of enforcing the rules.

7

The Rulemakers

IT'S DECEMBER 2017, and Ajit Pai is dancing.[1] A middle-aged man with closely cropped hair, wearing a suit – though no tie – Pai is awkwardly waving a lightsaber and dancing to the 'Harlem Shake', an out-of-date dance meme set to a song released more than five years before.

Pai's companions on the dance floor, four millennials, raise further questions. They are employees of the Daily Caller, a hard-right US political website with connections to the USA's white supremacist movement, and a track record of pushing dangerous and often incoherent conspiracy theories – including the notorious Pizzagate conspiracy, which alleged senior Democratic officials were using code words such as 'cheese pizza' in their emails to cover up a paedophile ring in which they were members.[2, 3]

The woman dancing next to Pai in his YouTube clip – which he had deliberately uploaded on the internet with the intention of going viral, this was no secretly recorded footage – was Martina Markota, who had herself recorded a video endorsing the insane conspiracy theory, which had led to an armed man forcing his way into a DC pizzeria, demanding to be allowed into its (non-existent) basement dungeon.[4] Thankfully, no one was hurt.

Markota opens her Pizzagate video talking about testimony from a woman who she described as 'an ex-CIA sex slave' who in the 1990s had accused Hillary Clinton of being a lesbian involved in trafficking sex slaves – and then talking about the 'really, really fascinating' links between that and the 'Pizzagate stuff', with its code words. When 'her source' had told her one of those code words was 'cheese pizza', her eyes had lit up – she'd heard that code word in connection to this conspiracy before, she said.

Her conspiracy-stoking drivel continues for nearly seven minutes.[5]

It seems questionable why anyone would want to release footage of themselves awkwardly dancing with a group of figures from a website tied to the far right and to some of the internet's most bizarre conspiracy theories. It becomes particularly weird when you know who Ajit Pai is, and what he was overseeing that week.

Since his appointment by Donald Trump earlier that year, Pai was in office at the helm of, in his words, 'an agency that regulates one-sixth of the economy'[6] – including the internet itself, at least within the United States. Because Ajit Pai is the chairman of the Federal Communications Commission (FCC).

Founded during Franklin D. Roosevelt's tenure as president, the FCC is one of the USA's most powerful regulators – not only does it have oversight over the radio, television and phone industries, it also oversees all forms of interstate communications. This puts it into some of the most hot-button cultural issues of the country, from media ownership to broadcast regulations – but also gives it considerable oversight over broadband and internet rules in the United States. And the chair of its politically partisan board is selected by none other than the president.

Like many Trump appointees to regulatory and oversight roles, Pai entered his role as FCC chair as a known deregulator, who had previously worked briefly in the industry which he would now oversee – serving for a time in the counsel's office for Verizon, and also as a DC-based communications lawyer, prior to serving as an FCC commissioner.

The early months of Pai's term saw several decisions benefiting media friendly to Donald Trump – a move Pai and his allies insisted was purely coincidental. In April 2017, the FCC passed a series of moves – after extensive industry lobbying – to relax ownership restrictions on networks buying up more local television stations.[7]

The result gave Sinclair Broadcast Group, a pro-Trump Conservative network, in particular a lot more latitude for purchases, and soon after the group announced a $3.9 billion merger deal with the media and newspaper group Tribune.[8] A few months later, the group – which was still waiting for its deal to be cleared by other regulators – attracted considerable media attention, after forcing dozens of local news anchors to read on-air identical scripts condemning media bias and 'false news', to the tweeted delight of Donald Trump.[9]

The decision Pai – whose media team did not respond to requests for an interview for this book – was building towards in December 2017, though, was a far bigger one with potentially global ramifications. Pai was preparing for a meeting in which his committee would vote on whether to repeal strict rules governing how cable companies and other internet service providers handled the traffic on their network – referred to as net neutrality principles, and for many as near to sacred as anything gets on the internet.

Rather than consulting experts or trying to build a consensus, Pai posted his video – '7 Things You Can Still Do On the Internet After Net Neutrality' – on the Daily Caller, illustrated by him in 3D specs, a Santa costume, a fidget spinner and a toy rifle, and – of course – by dancing the Harlem Shake.

Days later, his committee voted 3–2 – down party lines – to weaken the USA's rules protecting net neutrality. The result was an online shouting match in all directions, which has not even begun to die down, months and years later.

IF THE IDEA of net neutrality is treated as sacrosanct by so many people who campaign for it, it's because it does seem to grow out of the very earliest principles of the internet and what made it different from the telecoms networks which came before.

On the internet, traffic was traffic, no matter what it was going between or whether it was an email, file transfer or something else. This was very different on other earlier networks – so, for example, attaching an answerphone to a US phone network could incur an additional charge, even if it didn't really make any difference to the amount of traffic on that network.

The core principle of net neutrality, mercifully, is a simple one: all traffic on the internet should be treated the same, no matter where it comes from, and no matter what type of data it is. This idea stems right from ARPANET, and the idea of breaking up whatever you're trying to transmit – text, photo, video or audio – into 'packets' of data, sending those, and having them reassembled at the other end.

The net neutrality principle is that a packet is a packet is a packet – none get priority, and none get held up. Part of the reason people get so intense about this as a principle, though, doesn't centre on abstract philosophy. It centres on what you can do if you throw this principle away.

The fear comes from what telecoms and cable companies do on other networks, where they're not barred from discriminating between different kinds of traffic – charging extra for any kind of premium service. If your cable company can identify which traffic coming to your device is HD video content, it could offer you a 'premium package', allowing you to have internet plus HD streaming for just £5.99 a month extra. If it detects your traffic is from Facebook, Twitter and Snapchat, it could offer you a 'social package' with unlimited social networking for just an extra £2.99.

This could go further. Let's imagine your telecoms provider is also the company which provides your internet. Would it really want to let you use services like Skype or Facetime, rather than using your minutes, or paying as you go? Without a principle enforcing net neutrality – in essence forcing the pipework behind the network just to be 'dumb pipes' that send and receive whatever they get – this would be legally possible.

Beyond that still, activist groups warn that if the infrastructure needed to analyse each packet as it travelled and looking into its contents became normal, tyrannical governments could easily make use of it to restrict access to content, control the internet and tighten their hold on power. Such things are already possible, but losing net neutrality could normalise it and reduce its cost.[10]

No wonder, then, that when the tech blog Gizmodo – known for its snark, and an outlet with a clear pro-net neutrality stance – covered Ajit Pai's promotional video for his forthcoming FCC decision it was decidedly blunt.

'If passed, the FCC would allow ISPs to begin setting up a tiered internet designed to suck as much money from customers' pockets as possible while screwing with their ability to access competitors' content, or really anything that might suck up amounts of bandwidth inconvenient for their profit margins,' the article noted. 'He's trying to buy precious cover by painting everyone who disagrees with him as a simple-minded idiot.'[11]

One man with a ringside seat of the row is former FCC chair Tom Wheeler, Ajit Pai's immediate predecessor. Wheeler, who was appointed by Barack Obama, has had to watch his successor systematically and gleefully dismantle many of the achievements of his tenure – including the tighter net neutrality rules his FCC passed in 2015.[12]

Wheeler, though, hardly entered the FCC as an anti-industry hippie: he had spent a good chunk of his career working as a lobbyist for either the cable industry or wireless companies – and then he swapped sides. Wheeler tells me he thinks this gave him a certain dose of scepticism, as well as a dose of history – he could recall when the industry was crying out to be classed as 'common carriers', regulatory code for a network serving the general public, which would be covered by FCC rules, rules they're now trying to have relaxed.

'Well, the fun thing was that I was working for the cable industry and a wireless industry but they were all the insurgents,' he says. 'They were trying to take on the incumbents. The cable industry was challenging the three broadcast networks as well as the telephone company, and the wireless industry was taking on the wire industries. I thought that what I was doing was pro-competitive and pro-consumer, because we were giving consumers choices and expanding competition. The reality then becomes, of course, that as companies move from insurgent to incumbent their perspectives change ... And so I then got to deal with those same companies at the other stage of their growth. Then I was their regulator! I had been on the inside, I understood.'

He recalls being told during the network neutrality row hearing that being 'common carriers' and keeping net neutrality was destroying the ability of cable companies to invest in essential infrastructure.

But he remembers being a lobbyist for that same industry in the 1990s, and briefing on behalf of cable companies asking to be made into 'common carriers', otherwise they wouldn't be able to invest, as they wouldn't have stable rules to follow.

'I'm sitting there and I'm listening to these arguments and I'm saying, "No, wait a minute, which one of these is right?" We looked back and after they were made common carriers in '93, they spent something like $300 billion in investment. Well, it doesn't seem as though it hurt 'em!'

Wheeler is now a vocal advocate for net neutrality, and under his chairmanship the FCC eventually passed the historic expansion of net neutrality protections which Pai revoked in December 2017. He was not always perceived as such – in the early days of his tenure, given his industry history, he was seen as a potential opponent of it, only to be converted to the cause.[13]

'I knew what I wanted to accomplish,' he says now. 'There was debate over what's the best way to accomplish it, but there wasn't a moment's hesitation that we wanted fast, fair and open networks.'

Wheeler spent years consulting, holding meetings and developing his thought before strengthening net neutrality rules towards the end of his tenure. Pai took a different approach, opening the FCC site to online comments, in line with its rules, but seeming as if he had already opted to revoke yet another Obama-era landmark decision.

The resulting row and story almost served as the internet in microcosm. A regulatory row – seen by cynics as a simple case of corporation versus corporation, whether the rules favour YouTube, Netflix and co. or the cable giants – rapidly escalated, with accusations of Russian interference, of bot armies, of DDoS attacks, of corrupt corporate power and more.

The public craziness started with John Oliver, the host of *Last Week Tonight*, who had spoken out in favour of net neutrality on the show in 2014, ahead of the Obama-era considerations of the issue. He did so again in May 2017, warning that Ajit Pai's proposals 'would make net neutrality as binding as a proposal on *The Bachelor*'[14] – and urging his viewers to go to www.gofccyourself.com (an address the show deliberately set up to point to the real FCC's website) and leave an official comment on the plans.

Oliver can mobilise an audience – there was a huge rush to give feedback against the proposals to curb net neutrality, but many viewers were unable to leave any comment, as the FCC's website promptly crashed. FCC officials, including Pai, blamed deliberate DDoS attacks against its website for the outage – a line seen as a weak excuse by net neutrality supporters, who felt the agency was looking for excuses for failing to keep its site online for feedback, especially when it was feedback the FCC chair didn't seem to want.

Around a year later – long after the final decision – the truth emerged: there had been no hacking attack, and the FCC's site had fallen over in response to a flurry of real demand from John Oliver's viewers. Moreover, Pai had been aware of this for many months, but had not publicly revealed it, and had even stuck with his original story – to allow for a potential prosecution against the IT official who had wrongly attributed the attack, he said.[15]

That was far from the only controversy during the feedback process – the FCC found itself bombarded with responses from fake names, comments submitted in the name of deceased Americans and disposable email addresses.

On the eve of the FCC's decision, the then New York Attorney General Eric Schneiderman issued a statement revealing around 2 million comments on the net neutrality proposals were fake. He called for a delay to the process, to try to deduce the real balance of opinion. 'Moving forward with this vote would make a mockery of our public comment process and reward those who perpetrated this fraud to advance their own hidden agenda,' he said.[16]

The vote took place the next day.

In the following months the FCC blocked all attempts to find out who had been behind the campaign to bombard the agency with millions of fake comments – refusing multiple requests for data from the New York AG, and refusing multiple freedom-of-information lawsuits from journalists.[17] Pai even turned the fake comments to his own advantage after being accused of facilitating a 'cover-up' by one of the Democratic FCC commissioners.

In a decidedly snarky public response to the request for records and to his FCC colleague, Pai complained the commissioner said 'a lot' about the process, but ignored 'the fact that the half-million comments submitted from Russian e-mail addresses and the nearly eight million comments filed by e-mail addresses from e-mail domains associated with FakeMailGenerator.com supported her position on the issue!'[18] He did not back up his claim, but it was enough to prompt a wave of headlines about Russian interference in the FCC process – despite Russian emails being a fairly standard spam technique, proving nothing about who might be behind the attack, despite Pai's apparent insinuation.[19]

Overall, though, it hardly seemed to matter what anyone – real or fake – thought of his plans: Pai seemed set to just do what he wanted anyway. Even when detailed polling produced by the School of Public Policy of the University of Maryland, which gave balanced information for and against Pai's proposals, showed 75 per cent of Republicans and 89 per cent of Democrats opposed them,[20] he was unmoved, dismissing it as 'biased'.[21]

Who, then, were Ajit Pai and his two fellow Republican FCC commissioners listening to when they made their decisions on net neutrality? For Tom Wheeler, the answer is obvious – Donald Trump's administration has sided with industry over users.

'The Trump FCC is marching entirely to a drumbeat that is set by the industry,' he says. 'The stakes are huge. They're making the rules for the most important network of the twenty-first century. Period.'

Because of those stakes, Wheeler notes, industry has got very good at influencing both the FCC and Congress – which ultimately oversees the FCC's work and which can often either steer it in the right direction or legislate in helpful ways outside the FCC's direct remit.

'The FCC is an interesting animal,' he muses. 'It is a creature of Congress, yet it has a majority of the president's party. Remember, I've played both sides of the street. The way in which you influence the FCC is through those two pathways. Sure, you participate in the formal straightforward proceedings of the FCC, but in particular, you bring pressure to bear from out of Congress. The networks are incredibly effective in their ongoing relationships with Congress, but it's beyond just their lobbying. One of the other things they do very, very effectively is they have set up a whole series of allegedly independent groups. So-called think tanks that can always be counted on to parrot their line. So-called independent consumer groups, or ethnic groups that they support and that follow their lines. You're constantly confronted with "Well, here's a new economic study that is biased in the assumptions it makes, and therefore biased in the results that it produces", or this group or that group standing up and saying, "This is going to be bad for whomever it may be." That's just the process.'

Wheeler ultimately now has something of a physical view of the internet – at least so far as the FCC is concerned – and keeps his focus beyond the people who already have a strong view on net neutrality, to those who might never have heard of it, but who in his opinion rely on it. For him, the internet is a utility like electricity, gas or water.

'You never talk about the pipes, you talk about whether the water tastes funny,' he says. 'But I think that everything has to start with the networks. The networks that connect us are the force that defines us, because if we can't connect, then there's not going to be any Facebook, there's not going to be any Google. Unfortunately, we are existing in an environment where, technically, high-speed broadband networks are local monopolies, and monopolies operate in order to advantage themselves and to exploit their monopoly position. It just seems to me that there ought to be some kind of a countervailing force in there speaking on behalf of consumers and competition.'

THE FCC, OF course, is just one regulator among many. The challenges of regulating the internet giants in practice, though, are numerous. For one, the companies are so big and so wealthy that even the world's largest authorities will quickly find themselves outspent and out-lawyered – and at least until recently, the authorities were risking the ire of public opinion by going against popular businesses, which had done well positioning themselves as consumer champions.

In addition, internet companies are often working in new areas and new ways, outside the scope of existing regulation. They also have the ability – unlike bricks-and-mortar companies – to operate in a country with virtually no physical or financial footprint in it, meaning that only the biggest markets can hope to hold them to account.

All of these factors, coupled with the technical complexity of the internet and the fact many key components in its firmament are virtually ungoverned, has meant that the rulemakers lag far, far behind the technology giants – whether the cable companies or the content ones. The only markets currently big enough to credibly build authorities that could hold them to account are, at present, the EU and the USA, with the potential for a rising China to become the third – with all the free speech and transparency issues that creates.

There is, though, an extra dilemma facing one of those: the USA is conflicted. Given it controls so many of the world's internet giants, is it really in its interest to hold their power to account?

That's a question which Emily Bell, director of the Tow Center for Digital Journalism at Columbia University, is keen to consider, after years of tracking the online landscape and looking at how different regulators react to the Twitters, Googles and Facebooks of the world. She sees the online world with a very US-centric and US-inspired culture, which may have held regulators there in check.

I meet Bell in her uptown Manhattan office, in the middle of Columbia's journalism school, where she immediately opens by explaining why she believes regulation is so antithetical to big tech.

'I've always said the problem with big tech was that you got the engineering model of Stanford University lashed to the economic model of Chicago University,' she explains. 'You basically got the free-market Friedmanites as an economic model, and then you have a theory of zero latency engineering.'

Bell is referring to the ultra-free-market reasoning that grew out of the Chicago School of Economics – a school of thought that came to dominate the world and influence the economic policies of Ronald Reagan in the US and Margaret Thatcher in the UK. This economic theory reasoned that markets were the best source of information and of value, and so obstacles to them – regulation, competition policy and other barriers – were usually impediments to that.

In big tech, Bell says, this economic orthodoxy – even if it is masked with a socially liberal culture – is fused with a technological mindset of zero latency, or moving as fast as you can and fixing things as you go along. The two for her are more dangerous together than they are individually.

'The two of them are fused, essentially, by venture capital,' she continues. 'To me, that's always looked like a disastrous marriage because it relies on a lack of regulation and essentially I'm a fan of regulation … It's also not their fault because they were just allowed to do it. I think they were allowed to do it, encouraged to do it,' she says, moving on to regulators' willingness to let Facebook buy up would-be rivals as an example. 'There was no regulation that said, "Hang on a second, we understand where this is going. Really you shouldn't be able to buy Instagram and you shouldn't be able to buy WhatsApp." There's some really basic things that could have happened that would have slightly changed the trajectory of this.'

Part of this can easily be explained by the USA's relatively relaxed – as compared to Europe, at least – competition rules, which tend to be more corporation-friendly and which will often allow companies to grow to a huge size, provided no one can demonstrate its scale is directly leading to higher prices for consumers – which in the case of a free-to-users service like Facebook is, in the short run anyway, entirely moot.

But Bell draws on a second explanation: if big tech is consolidating power across the world, and influencing culture across the world, it is clearly a component of US soft power – thus creating a conflict of interest for the US, which may be tempted to allow these companies to grow to a huge worldwide scale for its own strategic advantage.

'When we talk about regulation, regulation of Google, regulation of Facebook, you always have to think about what is the national security and the defence angle to this, because they are not just companies. They are actually part of the soft power of America over the rest of the world. The idea that a model of regulation won't reflect this at some point is hopelessly naive, I think … It's the history of Silicon Valley. The history of Silicon Valley is the defence industry, it was the defence industry in America in the fifties and sixties. It has been commercialised, but that has never gone away, as the culture that says, this actually has a relationship with central government … It is not just the Silicon Valley companies. Places like AT&T, all these places have research labs, R&D labs. Many of those would have had government funding, NSF grants, et cetera. DARPA funds research through all these things. They're not doing it for fun.'

That's a broad international geopolitics argument as to why the US has not moved quickly to try to govern the online world or to hold the huge new corporations it has created in check. But Bell has an argument on a much more domestic scale, too – looking at the people who the new online businesses have actually disrupted.

It's disputable that the internet has disrupted the people in power – and the closer we examine it, the less convincing that idea seems. But that doesn't mean the internet hasn't been disruptive, it just means instead that the people who are most disrupted are virtually invisible to most politicians and regulators, and so carry very little clout.

'Here is what I think it has changed,' Bell says. 'I think it's disempowered people as much as it's empowered them. One of the things that it did was undermine the basis of organised labour and say, "Unions pfft, organised labour, pfft." I think that's what we're going through now. Which is, "Did it disrupt much?" "Yes!" Go and talk to African American women in the Midwest who are all losing their jobs because of retail and Amazon. Go to any small town that is not on the coast and see what tech has done.'

Given the pace of technological change in the online era – much faster than previous such revolutions – catching up with regulation could take far, far longer than almost anyone would expect.

'The fact it moves so much faster means that you have this massive period of change, which in the Industrial Revolution was about fifty to a hundred years,' she says. 'It then has to be followed by fifty to a hundred years of social reform. Actually, when you think about how what happened in the early to mid-twentieth century, a lot of that was about social reform, educational reform, health-care reform – which had to be built on top of the chaos wrought by the Industrial Revolution.'

After setting out these fifty-to-a hundred-year timelines for previous technological revolutions, Bell notes we have had less than twenty years since the first dotcom boom.

Finally, when the formal safeguards of society – regulators, lawmakers and the courts – fail to keep up with change, fail to act for some other reason, or even fail to see a problem, there are supposed to be informal mechanisms in society that step up to the bar and help at least highlight problems and hold power to account.

Two of the most obvious of these are academia and journalism. One is supposed to research the issues in depth; the other serves as a 'first draft of history', an occasionally crude attempt to draw attention to what might be wrong.

In both cases, it can certainly be argued that sceptical coverage and scrutiny of technology has increased – but it can also be argued that the sector has done brilliantly in neutralising these watchdogs. One way is simply through telling a good story that reporters want to hear – the scrappy upstart, the disruptor, the college dropout who built a business and showed everyone who knew best. Everyone likes an underdog story.

But as the tech companies have grown, they have got good at neutralising potential independent scrutiny. In academia, they can offer to hire the best and the brightest, for far more money than a university could ever match. Otherwise, they can offer to fund labs and share their data only with academics that show the right attitude – and if you don't like it, they can always take the unique and valuable dataset they were offering elsewhere.

'I think that big tech companies buy out dissent, easily buy out dissent,' Bell says. 'Google, Facebook, Apple, whoever, are all over computer science departments, et cetera. If you are a top academic working in, say, facial recognition or neurolinguistic programming [a controversial academic approach to communications and mental health], just pick something at the moment, the idea that your salary would be twenty times what it is – and people are not badly paid in institutions like this – and that these people will make your research easier, they will give you the data, too. If you're not prepared to take it, you're shut out because they don't really want independent enquiring into what they're doing. And it's the same for journalism.'

Given the well-advertised working conditions for their employees – lots of autonomy, huge salaries, great perks – even internal dissent is rare. The senior staff and the boards that the top CEOs surround themselves with, Bell concludes, are a lot like them. And it shows, she says, citing Mark Zuckerberg again as an example.

'He has a governance panel on his board which is Peter Thiel [PayPal co-founder and VC], Marc Andreessen [Opera co-founder and VC] and Reid Hoffman [LinkedIn co-founder and VC],' she says. 'You have three extremely rich white men, who've all made their money from similar areas and all of them have an incredibly narrow view of the world, who are Facebook's governance.'

TOM WHEELER, WHO'S now a visiting fellow at the Brookings Institute, the Washington DC think tank, has been trying to place the internet revolution in its proper place in the long view. Like Bell, he sees parallels to previous technological revolutions – but he also sees the potential for the internet to have worked very differently from, say, railways, which has not yet materialised.[22]

'Historically, networks have been centralising forces,' Wheeler explains. 'The railroad, the classic example which created the Industrial Revolution, centralised production by hauling the raw materials to a point where they could be produced on a mass scale and joint economies scale, and then redistributed out to an interconnected population.'

Wheeler has volunteered the same railways comparison Wenger offered – but is driving at something a little different. His argument is that it costs a lot to build a railway to a particular place, but once it's there it doesn't cost much to run another train – and it certainly doesn't cost much to add an extra freight carriage to an existing train. That means it makes sense to produce and haul a lot of one particular good for one particular destination, in a way that it didn't before – one horse and cart can take a certain amount, and more costs the same again.

'Everything was centralised,' Wheeler continues of the industrial age. 'Why is steel in Pittsburg? Why are cars in Detroit? Why are grain and slaughterhouses in Chicago? It was all because of the early impacts of the railroad and their centralising force, because you had to come to Chicago to switch to get to a track leading to another place, so while you're there why not do something with your product?'

That's explicitly not how the internet works: as we have seen time and again it is by its design distributed, and at least in theory shouldn't have some central point at which things are forced to gather.

The problem, as we have seen in previous chapters, is that thanks to the decisions that were made around our data and who holds it, the platforms (the Googles and Facebooks of the world) became the virtual versions of Chicago, the gathering points that then become essential hubs – and now the people who own the physical infrastructure are scrabbling to break into that world too. In the online world, where you might imagine real estate was unlimited, there is a land-grab, of sorts.

In the TV era the cable giants had a huge degree of dominance, and a model based on being selective about what travelled on their networks. In the internet era, that model has been challenged, and they've seen the new, supposedly distributed internet create huge new centralised platforms.

'The networks themselves are wildly jealous of these, and are therefore trying to assimilate into them,' he says. 'Why did AT&T buy DirecTV? Why did they buy Time Warner, et cetera? They want to get into these platform activities … We have a ubiquitous distributed network that has created a new level of centralisation.'

That means that the old-school model even of a more enlightened and attentive FCC would not be enough: as the gap between the content companies, who make entertainment, and the cable companies, who transmit it, becomes smaller and smaller, something will have to be able to tackle both.

'Because the networks are typically local monopolies, we need to have oversight of them,' Wheeler concludes. 'Now, because of the fact that the platforms are using those networks to build network effects that create bottlenecks to affect the competition in platform services, we need oversight of the platform services as well.'

The joy and the wonder of the internet is that everything is connected. Clearly, for anyone trying to look at how to fix its problems, the fact that everything is connected makes every-thing a lot harder, too.

THE FINAL GREAT challenge for the rulemakers is that the internet is continuing to change so fast that even the rules that we do have and can enforce rapidly go out of date. We have discussed the fact that the internet isn't a 'cloud' – it is a network of cables, crossing countries and continents and enveloping the world, joining servers that hold our data.

That is changing. The so-called 'final mile', the last stretch of the internet that connects up our laptop, tablet or phone, is now often wireless – thanks to 3G and 4G. This is particularly the case in the developing world, which often never got the landline technology ubiquitous elsewhere, but which is now leapfrogging such technologies and jumping directly for mobile.

However, wireless technology as a primary source of connectivity is coming to the West, too – in the form of 5G, the impending successor to 4G which is being hyped as 'up to a thousand times faster' than existing mobile internet speeds. As ever, that theoretical maximum speed increase should be sensibly disregarded, but it really will be a lot faster, and, in a whole bunch of important ways, a lot smarter – to the point where it could easily replace home connections for many users.

That might just seem like a nice quality-of-life improvement, but behind the scenes it could make changes far more seismic than that. Airspace spectrum – bits of the wireless spectrum sold as '3G', '4G' or '5G' – is often treated differently to cable, and to other communications services, and during the process the companies developing their technologies in this space appear to have tried to strike and shift the rules on what could be possible, in ways that make hobbling net neutrality look quaint.

It is a risk the ICANN chief executive Göran Marby made a point of raising when discussing the dangers of handing control over Internet Protocols to others: they could use them for other motivations, whether political or commercial.

'Take 5G. In many of the 5G specs today, they talk about something called network slicing,' says Marby. Network slicing would essentially allow 5G to be broken up, or 'sliced', into smaller networks optimised for different apps or different types of content – designed to work ideally for video streaming, self-driving cars, industrial control information or some other form of content.

This has practical uses, but could easily be overextended to allow for the kind of charging by type of content that net neutrality was designed to prevent – if someone who stood to profit from it could say that video really does have technical needs different from those of instant messaging, they could maybe justify 'slicing' it, and then charging separately.

In theory, at least, some countries are trying to allow slicing only where it's 'essential' and not where it could impede free and equal access to the internet – this is the approach that the EU is trying to take, but legal experts who are looking ahead at this coming issue worry that the vagueness of the new terms creates scope for others to exploit.

Given that virtually any type of data or service can be transmitted via the internet, it is not clear what the 'services other than internet access services which are optimised for specific content, applications or services' allowed under the EU rules would be.[23] However fast regulators move – and it's usually slowly – the internet's land-grab seems faster.

The fight over 5G isn't just a US corporate one, though – and because it involves competition with China, it's one that has got the attention of President Donald Trump, a man not usually known for his close attention to technical details.

Across two tweets sent four minutes apart, Trump posted:

I want 5G, and even 6G, technology in the United States as soon as possible. It is far more powerful, faster, and smarter than the current standard. American companies must step up their efforts, or get left behind. There is no reason that we should be lagging behind on ...
[#]
... something that is so obviously the future. I want the United States to win through competition, not by blocking out currently more advanced technologies. We must always be the leader in everything we do, especially when it comes to the very exciting world of technology!

To many of the president's 59 million Twitter followers, his sudden interest in mobile spectrum technology – rather than job numbers, MAGA or building the wall – may have been cryptic, but Trump's tweets actually addressed a serious internal conflict within his own White House, exposing divisions between the pro-business wing and his national security advisers.[24]

The second group were looking for Trump to sign an executive order effectively banning Huawei, the Chinese hardware manufacturer with close ties to the country's government, from bidding to provide 5G to US cities. This was fuelled by fears that the company would use its provision of US internet to gain access to technological secrets and national security information, in much the way the US leveraged its own dominance of the wired internet to boost its own intelligence operations across the world, even if it did not engage in the same kind of intellectual property theft.[25]

Trump rejected this approach, preferring instead to spur on US companies to just win the technological race, rather than slowing the progress of the new technology – though as ever with Donald Trump, it is unclear whether or not this policy position will hold or be reversed. This is especially unclear as Huawei – which is locked in a bitter dispute with the US following the arrest on US orders of one of its senior executives as she travelled in Canada – issued what could be construed as something of a wind-up press response agreeing with Trump's tweet.[26] '[T]he US is lagging behind ...' Huawei chairman Guo Ping told Reuters. 'I think his message is clear and correct.'

Whatever the specific decision made by President Trump on Huawei and 5G – which constantly U-turned back and forth through 2019 as Trump continued his trade dispute with China – the development marks a significant tidal shift in the age of the internet.

We have come to see that, almost always, online power reflects offline power, and in the offline world at least, the era of the USA as the world's only superpower is coming to an end – and it's China that is rising fastest to join it as a second superpower.

Huawei is not China's only tech behemoth. China has its own version of Amazon, eBay and Paypal, largely merged within the same company, Alibaba. It has its own search engine rival to Google, Baidu, which like Google is also diversifying into AI, self-driving cars, ad platforms and more. Its WhatsApp rival WeChat is owned by a company called TenCent, which is now investing in global social networking apps.

The Chinese tech giants are no longer content to operate solely in China.

The USA certainly exploited the soft power and intelligence advantages of its global domination of the internet and its largest companies. If China's influence over those networks grows, few doubt it would do exactly the same as an absolute minimum – and given its track record stealing and exploiting intellectual property, it would likely go much further.

If it's strategy that has kept the US inactive in tackling the issues that the internet has raised, that strategic balance may now be changing – and the USA's window to take the lead in harnessing and regulating the internet for the greater good could be closing. There's nothing like 'use it or lose it' to spur action: will the US take this opportunity to build a global coalition and take action?

The reason for inaction, of course, may not be strategic. Emily Bell has one more reason to offer as to why no one seems to have got around to tackling what could easily be framed as one of the most pressing issues facing our society and its future, in so many ways: ignorance.

'I think it's just people being illiterate about technology. It's actually the main thing,' she says. 'It's just that not enough people really understood the actual math and the way these things worked. The people who did have been saying since forever that this would happen, but that's a very small number of people, largely speaking to quite an elite and enclosed audience. There was no incentive to listen to them. They weren't making any money, and they were just sort of suggesting ways in which you would stop making money.'

Trying to talk people into making less money is a tough sell. But it's a pitch someone's going to have to make.

8

The Resistance

IN THE CENTRE of San Francisco is a public space dedicated to efforts to establish a free and fair system of international rules, for the betterment of mankind. The United Nations Plaza, installed in 1975, is a 2.6-acre open square at the heart of the city, with an elaborate fountain serving as a centrepiece to a monument to humanity's higher ideals.

In front of the fountain an inscription opens with: 'Whereas recognition of the inherent dignity and of the equal and inalienable rights of all members of the human family is the foundation of freedom, justice and peace in the world . . .' before recounting the Universal Declaration of Human Rights in full.

But if the square is supposed to serve as a symbol of the international order in the heartland of the technological revolution, it is far more on the nose than it could ever have been intended to be. The fountain is dilapidated, with much of the inscription near it worn to the point of unreadability. Several of its pumps have failed, leaving it half-heartedly pumping just a few jets of water – the very definition of uninspiring, especially when the fountain is surrounded by 'San Francisco Public Works' barriers, making sure everyone keeps away.

As a public space, the UN Plaza has for decades shown the ugly realities of San Francisco more than its high ideals. The area has long attracted hustlers, prostitutes, addicts and the city's homeless population.[1] Just twenty feet or so away from the fountain – and a mere stone's throw from some of the world's most desirable places to work – there is a 'mid-market pit stop' needle exchange.

A five-minute walk through the centre of San Francisco will take you past Dolby, then Twitter's San Francisco offices, and then City Hall. If you turn onto Eddy Street, the first thing you notice is an uptick in the tents and shopping carts of homeless people, making their makeshift beds for the day or night here in even larger numbers than the city's high baseline.

And then, next to a showroom and service and maintenance garage for Minis – available from \$99 a month to lease – is a nondescript four-storey building, with perhaps as good a claim as any other to be the home of the fightback against coercive control of the internet: the Electronic Frontier Foundation (EFF).

The not-for-profit's HQ stands in stark contrast to the internet's for-profit big names.

Apple's new headquarters, a few dozen miles down the road, is a 2.8 million-square-foot ring of custom-made glass, whose automated four-storey-high sliding doors weigh twenty tons each. Its centrepiece building alone will hold 12,000 employees, with others working from satellites around it, and the campus features a 1,000-seat amphitheatre for the company's iconic product launches. The campus is reported to have cost around \$5 billion and took eight years to construct.[2]

In 2018, Facebook expanded its Menlo Park campus to include a new building with a 3.6-acre rooftop garden, hundreds of forty-foot-tall redwood trees, extensive pathways, a 2,000-person events space, five new restaurant options and more than a dozen new bespoke works of art.[3] Google is currently building a 595,000-square-foot campus with world-renowned designer Thomas Heatherwick on the US West Coast,[4] while simultaneously building a 'landscraper' – an office longer than the city's tallest building – in London to serve as its UK headquarters.[5]

Big tech firms have tens or hundreds of thousands of employees, billions in revenues, even higher valuations, and the ultra-glitzy headquarters to show for it. The EFF's building, which resembles a converted town house, is located on a San Francisco side street. It has fewer than a hundred paid staff, and that headcount includes Mackey Bear, the staff mountain dog, who 'specializes in getting treats from interns, barking at Board members and peeing in front of visiting movie stars'.[6] And it works on a budget of less than $15 million a year.[7]

Cindy Cohn, a lawyer who has been the EFF's executive director since 2015, and who served as its legal director for fifteen years before that, walks me into her corner office and explains what brought her into the organisation as we sit down at her somewhat worn office table – a hand-me-down from the building's former tenants, Planned Parenthood, she tells me. Not much goes to waste here.

Cohn's connection to EFF dates right back to 1990; she had studied human rights law through law school, and been interested in that field. By virtue of living in the Bay Area, she fell in with a crowd of people involved in the early internet, before the World Wide Web. These included John Gilmore, an early Sun Microsystems employee, and John Perry Barlow, perhaps best known as the lyricist for the Grateful Dead.

Barlow, who died aged seventy in 2018,[8] became known through the 1990s as something of an internet visionary, seeing its potential – but also its risks.

'I honestly believe, without hyperbole, that the people in this room are doing things which will change the world more than anything since the capture of fire,' he told a room of technologists in 1994. 'We may be hurtling toward a future in which every single thing we do will be visible to the government, and as it is right now, anytime you make a financial transaction you smear your fingerprints all over cyberspace. This does not need to be the case; but it's going to take a lot of changing consciousness to have it be otherwise.'⁹

Barlow and Gilmore had become two of the EFF's three founders in the summer of 1990, following a raid on Steve Jackson, a games book publisher who had been targeted by police after being (apparently wrongly) accused of receiving a document about how the emergency 911 system worked. After finally having the case dropped, the publisher noticed his bulletin board messages and emails had been accessed, and wanted to take action.¹⁰ A movement was born.

That case – the Steve Jackson Games case – was the first to establish that email communications deserved the same protections as phone and postal communications, as before this point authorities hadn't even bothered seeking warrants before intercepting or seizing them. And it was the EFF who represented Jackson in the case.

Barlow, ever the poet, became the one most keen to advocate a utopian and liberal vision for the internet, one on which he did not want the world's established powers to encroach, as he eventually said in a now famous declaration of independence, delivered in Davos, Switzerland – the home of the elite's World Economic Forum – in 1996.

Governments of the Industrial World, you weary giants of flesh and steel, I come from Cyberspace, the new home of Mind. On behalf of the future, I ask you of the past to leave us alone. You are not welcome among us. You have no sovereignty where we gather.

We are creating a world that all may enter without privilege or prejudice accorded by race, economic power, military force, or station of birth. We are creating a world where anyone, anywhere may express his or her beliefs, no matter how singular, without fear of being coerced into silence or conformity.

Your legal concepts of property, expression, identity, movement, and context do not apply to us. They are all based on matter, and there is no matter here.[11]

Cohn says she saw much of what Barlow saw – that the internet held huge and exciting potential, but that it would need to be fought for.

'He would often say that part of the reason why he had to be so optimistic was that he wanted to get out ahead of the forces of darkness who were going to come,' Cohn recalls. 'He knew that was going to happen ... I think that's right. I also think he was a naturally optimistic guy. And I think it's still the case that more people have a chance to reach a bigger audience through the digital networks than ever before in the history of mankind. We've eliminated physical distance as a barrier to who you can talk to and how quickly you can talk to them. This has become so embedded in our lives, we don't even see it any more ... We could give people a voice who'd never had one before. I worked at the UN right out of law school, and did a report on the Philippines, and I was trying to figure out about some human rights violations in the Philippines and there was no way to get information. Now, we have problems about the fact that there is propaganda and information manipulation, but those problems only happen because you have information in the first place – and I thought that this could be an avenue where we can really bring human rights to more people, and it was fun. It's still fun. It's fun every day.'

It might be fun, but if the idea of a not-for-profit makes you think of a cute hippie gathering, you have the wrong idea of the EFF: despite its small size and small budgets, it gets things done.

Where other NGOs rely on donations from corporates, or from major foundations, the EFF mainly lives off subscriptions and donations from its 40,000 members.[12]

As to what it does with that money, Cohn has a short answer.

'I sue people for a living,' she says with a laugh. 'We sue the government all the time, and we sue them to get access to information. The Freedom of Information Act cases are a core part of what we do, because if you can't get the information out of the government you can't use it. We continue to sue the NSA about the tapping into the internet backbone, the spying they do, as well as the phone records and the internet metadata programs. We've got a couple of cases involving governmental entities that are operating on Facebook, but trying to act as if they're private entities, and they can block people. There's one against Texas A&M [the university] for banning reference to anything having to do with PETA [People for the Ethical Treatment of Animals] or animal cruelty from their Facebook page. We're pointing out you're a government body, you don't get to do that. Of course, we're supporting the biggest of those cases in Trump's Twitter case [in which the courts found the president was not able to block US citizens on the network while in office] that our friends the Knight Foundation[13] are doing. We have a bunch of patentee cases where we're supporting people who are fighting back against patent trolls. There's a lot of litigation.'

Given Cohn came to the EFF's executive directorship via a role as its general counsel and legal director, it's unsurprising litigation takes up so much of her time – but it's not all the EFF does in trying to fight for its vision of the internet.

As well as some conventional activism, the EFF builds its own technology to try to help activist users take privacy issues into their own hands. Its projects include Panopticlick 3.0, which tests how well your ad blocker and privacy tools are working – my browser was judged to have 'some protection against Web tracking, but it has some gaps'.[14] It ties in with Privacy Badger, a smart anti-tracking tool to keep you anonymous, which is intended to learn on the job as new trackers develop.[15] It can be used alongside HTTPS Everywhere, which tries to make sure browsers only use HTTPs, a more secure browsing protocol that makes traffic harder to intercept.[16] Another project, Certbot, is aimed at helping the flipside – enabling HTTPs for people running small websites, making their browsing harder for third parties to monitor.[17]

These kinds of tools work well for the small fraction of online users who are signed-up privacy activists, and who have a high degree of technical knowledge – but they will never be the solutions for the mass market or the mass user, which is why the EFF isn't just a tool-building organisation.

The aim of EFF action is often to try to set the limits of government power: restricting its power to monitor online communications, or to seize electronics, or to limit freedom of speech – which makes net neutrality a strange beast for the organisation, as one way or another it comes down to regulating the internet. As such, the EFF regularly sticks to its litigation approach, as much as advocacy on the issue. The reason, Cohn explains, is to prevent the issue simply turning into a case of content companies versus the ones which manage the infrastructure.

'Because we stand up for the users, what network neutrality is trying to fight against is the idea that your ISP can go to a website that you want to visit and say, "Nice website you got there, it'd be a shame if anything happened to it, but if you pay us money we'll make sure that our customers can have access to your website,"' Cohn explains. 'I don't think your ISP should hold you hostage, or charge for access to you. You pay them to have access to the whole internet, not the pieces of the internet that pay them payola, to make sure they load well. From a user's perspective, this gets missed sometimes because people are so busy talking like it's just the cable companies versus the websites. The cable companies and the websites are fighting over access to you, and you should have a voice in this and that's why we care.'

The problems this book uncovers seem to call for regulation as at least a first step in tackling the problems the internet has unleashed.

That's not necessarily the view of the EFF, though, and it's worth seeing why not – and remembering why that resistance to greater state control and more exists, and where it comes from. And given that many of the problems of the internet arise from state power, and from the state's desire to have more insight into the lives of their citizens, these cautionary notes should be kept in mind. One of those is that if Americans hate their internet connection – and its provider – one of the things to blame might actually be regulation.

'I try to gently point out to my friends who say there is a problem with Facebook that we need to regulate is that the broadband markets are highly regulated,' says Cohn. 'We have a worse problem with monopoly with broadband in the United States than we do with the social networks, and the search engines, and the other things. Certainly when it hits people's pocketbooks and it also hits the quality of their internet service. Americans freak out when they go to South Korea or even Europe now and see how degraded our internet connectivity is because the duopoly doesn't have much of an incentive to make it better.'

Cohn's view is that many of the potential ills of the internet – including government overreach – can be averted by preventing monopoly power and making sure users have the ability to choose between competing services. If regulation helps achieve that, then that's to the good – but that doesn't have to be taken as a given.

'Good regulation can do good things – the open internet, network neutrality, et cetera – but it isn't an end in itself,' she says. 'It really depends on who's in charge and what kind of rules they want to push, and they can make the world worse or better. That's why we tend to point toward trying to figure out what are the ways that we can prop up competition instead of should we regulate or not. I think "should we regulate or not?" is not an interesting question. How do we create competition? What levers, both regulatory and commercial, markets, laws and norms create more competition, to make it so that people can vote with their feet? The governmental issue is still there but I think if the governments have to deal with a dozen different entities as opposed to just two, you increase the chances of people deciding if they want to fight back, and things like that.'

Clearly for the EFF it's surveillance that is a defining issue – it was government overreach in hunting down a leaked document that led to the lawsuit which EFF was founded to fight. The organisation's sceptical world view as to the extent of US surveillance – and the use of the internet to slowly expand foreign intelligence powers to be used domestically – has been confirmed time and again, especially in the wake of the Snowden revelations.

Given that grounding, and given the confirmation that when the government is granted online power it tends to exploit it, the EFF's wariness around regulation and oversight is understandable, as is its ongoing focus in using this area as a basis for its litigation. And it's something that Cohn agrees is built into the very bedrock of the internet – and into the financial and political incentives of the people in power.

'The network allows consolidated control and tracking,' she says. 'For me, this starts with the NSA and law enforcement, and the tremendous boon that networks have made for surveillance, for the surveillers in the governmental realm. It's also been a big boon for the surveillance business model which is the advertising business model. This proposition that the more the advertisers know about you, the more they can sell you. They line up neatly, and that's really hard because it's true that the network lets that happen.'

Tackling this issue means tackling deep political challenges, on an international scale. But this huge issue is one she acknowledges has been hard to garner public attention towards so far – partly because browsing the internet feels like something safe and private. The intrusion is invisible.

'There is just a fundamental thing that happens when you're sitting in front of your screen – you think you're alone,' says Cohn. 'Figuring out the cause and the effect of what's going on in this thing that you really cannot see, literally cannot see, is always hard. Humans do a horrible job about this. Humans smoke cigarettes and later they get lung cancer … It's taken years for people to be able to be okay with that cause and effect and do something about it. The moment that your privacy is being violated or your information is being shared, it's not visible to you at all. The effects are not visible to you or, at least, traceable causation is not clear. It's easy to just be like, "I can't think about that. I've got to think about the traffic jam I'm in and not the things I can't see." '

Cohn also notes that virtually every government has made the same decision when it comes to the internet: to use it to improve their national security and surveillance abilities – some with good intentions of maintaining existing capabilities and trying to prevent terror attacks, some with the intention of increasing their stranglehold over power. Some want it for an edge on the world stage, and some are simply clinging to surveillance in a confused desire not to get left behind by technological change.

'This is one thing that they all agree on. There's no government who's decided that their job is to try to shine a light on this and help their citizens see the problem, because they want to be doing it to the rest of the world. Whether it's the Five Eyes [the US/UK/Canada/Australia/New Zealand spying alliance] or China or Russia, they all have a self-interest that's getting in the way of what I think is the interest of their constituency, their citizens or the world and human rights. All of them are conspiring to do this.'

The consensus of democratic governments to set these norms creates dangerous precedents across other countries, Cohn says – ones that she's at the forefront of trying to fight, and ones that create rare human faces to exemplify the consequences of the choices the people in power are making.

'We had a case that we handled called Kidane[18] versus government of Ethiopia, where we had a guy in Maryland, who had malware put on his computer that reported back to an IP address controlled by the government of Ethiopia,' she explains. 'He's Ethiopian by birth but through asylum a citizen in the United States and involved in the democracy movements. I brought straight up wiretapping. Somebody's listening in to your Skype calls. This is a serious offence in the United States, it's a felony. I couldn't get the US government to say, "Actually, we don't think a foreign government should be wiretapping our citizens." I couldn't get State Department perspective, I couldn't get the government to participate, and ultimately, the court held that because it's a sovereign it's immune.'

In other words, Cohn was pursuing a case in which a US citizen had his calls and communications intercepted on US soil – a situation it's almost impossible to imagine a Western government would be happy to just let slide if it had happened with older telephone technology. But not only would no US government body intervene or comment during the case, the court also held there was no cause for action – because it was a foreign government suspected of doing the interception. Cohn is right to call the situation mind-boggling – both the US executive and its judiciary appear to be sanctioning foreign governments to spy on US citizens with impunity.

'That sovereign immunity prevents US law from protecting US citizens in their own homes from being spied on by foreign governments. This is crazy,' she says. 'If there's anything that a government ought to do, it ought to protect you in your own home against an attack by a foreign government. Even libertarians agree on this. We couldn't get the court to see this as a problem. I think they're wrong. I think that history is going to flip at some point. I think that this is our work.'

Cohn has a refreshing streak of honesty (and humility) about her own – and, of course, others' – lack of success in making surveillance a priority for the public.

Part of the problem, she says, is that often for effective campaigning the only kind of story that works is one with a single victim who can point to tangible harm that's been done to them – and even then that usually isn't enough.

'We have to figure out better ways to get visualisation in these things. We have to get people out of the individual mindset, into the idea of groups, or our democracy. Requiring an individual narrator-protagonist with a single bad thing that happens to him, this story model isn't going to work for a lot of these problems. Unless we learn how to up our ability to tell these stories, we're never going to get people to see them as a problem. Even in the context of my guy, Mr Kidane, where I did have an individual narrative, I couldn't do it.'

This problem isn't just one that the general public have – it's one shared by would-be funders, too: too often, people think the questions about systems and architecture on the internet are technical ones, niche and nerdy issues, rather than significant ones about who wields power and who keeps it in check on the internet – undoubtedly a key public utility of the twenty-first century.

As the woman at the helm of one of the few organisations that actually does make this stuff its top priority, Cohn likens herself not to a superhero, or to the trust-busters of the early twentieth century, but to something more prosaic: an underfunded plumber.

'It's really hard. I joke sometimes that the EFF is the plumber of freedom. We're trying to get these clogs out of the way – and there's not a lot of money for the plumbers,' she says, exasperated. 'As a society who depends on these networks there ought to be more attention paid. Like philanthropy, where I can show up in most philanthropy circles and try to talk about network infrastructure. Their eyes just glaze over, yet all the people who they're supporting all round the world who are trying to do this kind of work depend on it.'

Cohn, though, will stay optimistic. Her two and a half decades at the front lines of these online battles – which have only seen the stage get larger and the stakes get higher – have not dented the optimism she shared with John Perry Barlow and others in the 1990s.

Just because the task ahead is a tough one doesn't mean it's a fight not worth having – especially if you keep the upsides of the internet in mind, something that can be easy to forget when daunted by the power and money arrayed against its promise.

'I think that it is still the case that more people have a chance to reach a bigger audience through the digital networks than ever before in the history of mankind,' Cohn says of the internet's upside. 'Even just the family that's spread out all across the world and can really have ongoing conversations with each other regardless of that. I think those things all still exist. They didn't go away. If anything, the greatest honour of any new power is that we don't even notice it any more.'

It's this quality of connection – especially international connection – which keeps Cohn and the organisation she leads wary of curbing speech, as some in the West call for as a response to mounting populism. Does the planet as a whole need more free speech, or less?

'We see it so much more when we work with people around the world,' she says. 'There are a lot of people around the world who are a little frustrated with the modern Western idea that people have too much free speech, because they're still trying to get their voices out. I think it is a bit inappropriate for people in the West to suddenly start deciding who gets to speak or not without regard to the fact that that is a death sentence for lots of people around the world.'

For Cohn, building that intrinsic understanding of the internet, what it does to power, and why online privacy matters – and why online intrusion is just as much of a violation as someone reading your post, your diary, or rifling through the contents of your house – could prove a generational thing.

Discussions of online privacy and safety in the media tend to casually refer to the current generation of teens and early twenties as having no expectation of privacy, given they've grown up in the social media era and are always online. This is actually not remotely backed up by evidence – the generation of online natives are both far more aware of their online privacy and more likely to take practical steps to protect it, even if they are largely willing to sacrifice it to use social networks and online services.[19]

Even at this pace of technological change, Cohn is happy to try to capture the next wave of decision-makers if she can't get at the ones in power today.

'Kids aren't thinking about the government so much, but they're definitely thinking about teachers, each other, parents,' she says, adding that this then gives her a way in.[20] 'Well, you can take those insights and you can then take them up ... There are plenty of kids who do get that the government might be one of their threats. The idea that all of the tools you use to protect yourself against prickly parents are the same ones you might use to protect yourself against the government if things go wrong – this is not a new observation. Also, I think that a lot of people who are not kids have missed the difference, missed what privacy really is. I think that what we're seeing from kids today is that privacy is about control, it's about power. Do you have the power to protect yourself from things? You can decide to be a very public person. You can decide being an exhibitionist can be completely consistent with caring about privacy, because you still decide which pieces you reveal and what you don't.'

The coming contest for those hearts and minds, then, is the EFF and co. on one side, trying to support what they believe is an instinct teenagers and young adults already have, against vested interests whose business model relies on encouraging them either that privacy doesn't matter or that they have no hope of retaining it in the new online era.

'Sadly, we've got a generation of advertisers now who have tried to convince everybody that you don't have any privacy, you should get over it and that that's a good thing and you should be happy about it,' she says. 'There are plenty of people who have given up, which is too bad. That's my job, to try to convince people that giving up isn't that great a thing.'

IF CINDY COHN represents a school of activism which operates by tackling the ills of the internet head-on, through activism and through litigation, Jimmy Wales exemplifies another kind of resistance – of building something that works very differently.

Wales is one of the founders of Wikipedia, the fifth-most visited site on the internet,[21] whose English-language version gets more than 8.2 billion page views per month.[22] In English alone, Wikipedia's encyclopedia now comprises more than

5.8 million articles, edited more than 880 million times, by more than 35 million registered users.[23]

It has reached this scale without raising any money from venture capital, without showing any adverts, and without making any money – it is a registered non-profit, it has encyclopedias in 301 different languages, and gets by on less than $100 million a year, which it raises through donations – for which it advertises for just a few weeks every few months.[24]

Wales, then, is a dotcom founder with many similarities to the others – a site operating on a global scale, with huge audience and numbers – and many differences. Not least, he says, that he's not a billionaire. Wales also has little day-to-day control over Wikipedia and its parent foundation, though his word carries a good deal of influence, and so he works more as an activist – championing, as it happens, many of the same causes as Cohn and EFF. Wales works opposing overly strict copyright laws, supporting net neutrality, warning of the dangers of surveillance or controlling the internet, and more.

The venue he chooses for our chat seems particularly suited to his incongruous role: on the one hand, it's an immaculately fitted-out private members' club in London's Mayfair. On the other hand, it's not a standard private club: it's the newly opened Conduit Club, launched, as *Vogue* described it, as 'a place where you are not the only one who thinks they can change the world; where you could bump into an ethical investment fund holder at the bar, a sustainable fashion designer in the library, or the head of an influential NGO on the dance floor'.[25]

We are surrounded, then, by young social entrepreneurs hard at work on their laptops, their memberships sponsored and subsidised by their older and wealthier peers. Oblivious to who is at the next table, one of the would-be entrepreneurs checks Wikipedia as Wales talks.

Wikipedia had initially launched as part of a for-profit company (the now-dormant web company Bomis, where Wales worked as CEO), without any particular business model in mind, and in the wake of the dotcom crash. As Wales tells it, the event that spurred it towards being not-for-profit and donor-backed was happenstance rather than a particular design.

In the summer of 2003, Wikipedia 'was just a thing I was doing on the side. It was part of the company,' Wales recalls. 'I decided that it made more sense to be in the non-profit structure – this was the depths of the dotcom crash really. There was no obvious business model at all. The volunteers really wanted it to be a non-profit. That made just an aesthetic sense to me, that it should be a shared global resource.'

It was a nightmare at Christmas that provided the necessary proof that donations could work to fund Wikipedia, which previously had received financial support from Bomis, until the dotcom crash necessitated pulling the plug.[26]

'We were running on three servers, a database server and two front-end web servers. Two of the three servers crashed on Christmas Day. By that time I had moved away from San Diego, but the servers were out in San Diego. My one employee who was still out there had gone home for Christmas. There was no way to actually physically do anything. I had to scramble on Christmas Day and get it all running on one server, which I did. Then, it was miserably slow, as you can imagine. We managed after Christmas to cobble something together. I realised actually we probably need a lot more servers. It'd been growing really fast. When it's slow, it doesn't grow and so on. That was when we did the first fundraiser. I hoped to raise $20,000 in the thirty days that are in a month. We managed to get $30,000 within a couple of weeks. That was a shocker. That was really amazing. For the first time, we had some real indication that that model would work because before that it was not clear how we were going to fund this.'

Going not-for-profit, as Wales tells it, wasn't particularly some huge act of altruism – it was the only way to get funding at a time when it was scarcer, especially for a project which was reliant on volunteers being willing to give their time and knowledge for free. Would they really do that for a project making millions for someone else?

'There was no obvious model and nobody had done anything quite like it – we were Web 2.0 before Web 2.0 as a term was invented. I didn't think Wikipedia should have advertising. I always opposed it. I never said no, but I always said, "I don't want it. We need to figure out what we can do." Also, for a volunteer project, it doesn't make sense to have a paywall model. I mean, really, the idea is a free encyclopedia for everyone in their own language, so it has to be free. It was very exciting to see, wow, actually people will support this. That was also crowdfunding before Kickstarter existed, and all of that.'

Wikipedia's model of creating content for free, and delivering to users for free, proved impossible to deal with – even when Microsoft, then still seen as an unstoppable juggernaut of the tech world, moved in on its turf, creating the ability for regular users to create entries for its still-popular *Encarta* encyclopedia.

'There was a point when they announced with great fanfare that they were going to allow people to edit in *Encarta*. That was a little … you're reading the press, "okay, this is nerve-racking". Then it was completely ludicrous. I signed up to edit something and you could take an article, you make some changes and you submitted. It would say, "Thank you. Our crack team of academics and researchers will get back to you, probably within a month." I was like, "That's it. I'm not worried. That's not going to change anything." '

The *Encarta* debacle ties into a broader issue for Wales – the business model a site or service follows will become inextricably connected to how it operates, and to its values. On a surface level, a service asking for people to volunteer their time for no reward is likely to struggle if it works as a for-profit, unless the volunteers are getting something back – but the indirect effects of this connection can become much more far-reaching.

Wales cites the example of looking at how sites stand up to decisions such as censorship, or handing over information, to autocratic countries. If you don't have to worry about loss of revenues there, that gets easier. If you know that your user base will rebel against you if you do the wrong thing, it becomes easier still.

'My belief is that organisations naturally follow the money,' he says. 'Even if there are certain principles that you adhere to, if your business model is in conflict with those principles, then, over time, it's very hard to keep an organisation on principle … That is true for profits and non-profits. It's why we see a lot of bad NGOs, whose business model is based around pretty brochures for donors in the West rather than actually solving problems.'

Wales cites the case of Wikipedia and Turkey as a specific example of how Wikipedia's business model supports its principles. Turkey has blocked the encyclopedia within its borders due to pages accusing the country of acting as a state sponsor of terrorism, owing to alleged funding to ISIS and al-Qaeda. These pages violate Turkey's communications laws.[27] Wikipedia was not only able to stand its ground during the censorship row, Wales said, but it had to, or else its users and donors would turn on it. The result, he said, keeps the site honest.

'Right now, we're currently blocked in Turkey,' he says. 'People are like, "That's such a brave and principled stand. You don't cave in." I'm like, "Yes, it is," except it's also 100 per cent consistent with our business model, in the sense that we're a charity that depends on the public to donate money. We know that our donors appreciate our stance on these issues. If we said, "Yes, we're actually going to delete a few pages because they offend the Turkish government," our donations are going to crash. It's going to kill us. It would be appalling ... Being a non-profit helps us have that view. Also, it helps us have the view in the sense that, well, it's not like I'm giving up my yacht because of not having business with Turkey. I don't have a yacht anyway.'

This doesn't mean Wikipedia is perfect – nothing is. The site has many of the same gender-bias problems as the rest of the internet: 90 per cent of the site's volunteer editors – who work remotely to build and supervise the site's entries – identify as male, and only 9 per cent as female,[28] and female editors have complained about online harassment and abuse on the site.[29] This is reflected in the site's coverage: while more than half the people in the world are women, women make up fewer than 18 per cent of the site's biographical articles.[30] And in an online environment where misinformation – and the fear of it – is rife, experts have warned of Wikipedia's potential for exploitation in this sphere too.[31]

Wikipedia is not immune to the problems of the internet – but its not-for-profit model does shelter it from some of the conflicts of interest, and some of the moral ambiguities faced by Facebook, Google and others.

'I do think that these companies are struggling,' Wales says. 'With Facebook, the business model drives them to do things that the public isn't really liking and, I think, a lot of internal people at Facebook are probably not liking. Geeky engineers tend to have quite good views on these kinds of things, and yet it's hard for them to pull back from certain things.'

For Wales, it's the open internet and its spirit of experimentation and connectedness that has made what he's built possible – even if elsewhere we have seen the dangers of building infrastructure on the fly. If you're building a site or service, rather than the protocols that power the actual fundamentals of the network, the playful approach can work out better all round.

Wales sees a period in the internet of the late 1990s and early 2000s when things could have gone very differently, in a way that would have made today's net neutrality arguments seem like small fry. This was the era when a few of the largest internet service providers – in those days, AOL and CompuServe – were trying to create their own platforms to keep users looking at content they created and curated, over which they had near-total control.

'I actually feel like we dodged a bullet, a really big bullet, which was just when the internet began to really flourish and grow, and become a diverse ecosystem. You had AOL, CompuServe, Prodigy, these big providers that were complete walled gardens of a kind we can't even conceive of now. There was a good argument to be made that, because of network effects, one of them would be the winner ... You would get ten AOL CDs a week. They were flooding the whole planet with CDs.'

At the time, you wanted to be on AOL because that was the easiest way to message your friends and share the same services. It seemed to have the momentum.

'It's the classic argument of you need to be on AOL because that's where all your friends are. Once that hill starts to go, it's very hard to break out of that, which is exactly what people say about Facebook now.'

'Possibly it would be too hard for one company to create and allow the innovation on the platform of diverse services. You can imagine how hard it would be for Wikipedia to survive if it had to work with AOL, probably pay a licence fee to even get on the platform. It's a whole different model. The alternate model was just an explosion of creativity that drew people away.'

We are, Wales says, lucky to have avoided that walled garden, AOL-ised internet, and thus AOL-ised world. Unless we didn't. Recalling a talk from the Harvard law professor and respected internet thinker Jonathan Zittrain,[32] Wales suggests we might not have got as far away from the old AOL walled gardens as we'd like to imagine.

'He did this great speech where he showed the home screen of AOL and CompuServe – a series of icons,' Wales says. 'He's like, "Fortunately, we passed this in the wild, open web and there's all these things. Nobody needs permission to do anything." He's like, "Now we have the cellphone." Then he shows the screen. It's like BANG. We're back. it's CompuServe again. This company controls everything you're able to do on here. You have to pay the fee to be on there. Very interesting.'

The controlled app world of Apple and Android has some benefits for users – it protects against viruses, and to an extent against dodgy apps and scams, but it does it at the price of experimentation, and against freedom of control (and fee-skimming) from the phone manufacturer or the phone networks, or both. It doesn't, Wales says, let you play – and playing is where lots of good ideas start.

'Something like Minecraft. Minecraft grew out of a clever guy on a forum with a bunch of gaming geeks, going, "Hey, I made this little game. What do you think?" They give him feedback. He changes it and so on. That just doesn't happen in the app world.'

As for Wales himself, does doing the right thing – even if you do experiment and play – mean giving up all prospects of being dotcom-founder levels of successful? Wales's own fame suggests it needn't mean giving up fame or public profile, but as he notes, he is not a billionaire.

He is, though, no one's idea of a pauper, either. While the core of Wikipedia operates as a not-for-profit, Wales also helms a for-profit variant of the site, based on the same technology, and displaying adverts. Fandom allows fanbases of video games, TV shows and more, to create their own specialist Wikipedia-like sites to follow the intricacies of their particular fan universe in often unbelievable detail.

Wales's activism might be the most visible sign of his resistance to the dominant forces of the internet, but it's Wikipedia itself that's the most obvious challenge to how things are usually done. Wikipedia doesn't rely on intrusive advertising or tracking, it didn't need huge amounts of venture capital money, it hasn't made anyone ultra-rich, and it relies on a community that has to be fostered rather than exploited. It's not perfect – nothing is – but it's become one of the largest sites on the internet with a model like none of its rivals.

And it doesn't seem to have come at too high a price. As Wales said, he doesn't have a yacht – and I'm happy to take his word on that – but he isn't doing without altogether.

'I have a twenty-three-foot speedboat, a family speedboat in Florida,' he admits. 'I'm fine.'

Conclusion

THIS BOOK HAS been about trying to tell the story of the internet – of how it really works, and who really benefits from that. It's been about trying to turn a story we are told is technical, is boring, is something we don't need to worry about and that we can safely ignore, into something more human.

Because it is a human story. Any story about power and wealth always is. The internet is the product of a long chain of human decisions and incentives. It is not some outside force imposed upon us. But what's striking is how much it feels like that, even to the people within this book who helped make it what it is today.

The internet has only just entered its sixth decade: there are 1.7 billion people alive on the planet who were born before its invention.[1] It's only been a mass phenomenon for twenty years. Many of its biggest companies are still run by the people who founded them; much of its architecture was built by people who are still alive and looking at the effects of what they began.

And yet almost none of them feel like they're in control. But that's just how technological change works. The people who built the internet's infrastructure say the huge global network today doesn't feel like the result of what they built – but it is. This is what their insight tells us about its relationship to power, whether corporate or governmental.

Steve Crocker, and the records from his contemporaries and DARPA, showed us that the origins of the internet were the product of several different groups with very different motivations: senior academics who could only have funding to network computers, not buy more; their junior colleagues, seeing potential many of their supervisors missed, seizing an opportunity to go well beyond their brief; and a US defence research agency wanting a low-risk space to test networking technologies before it unleashed them on national security infrastructure.

ARPANET was overseen by the US Department of Defense for much of its first two decades, and then – even if at arm's length – by the Department of Commerce for another two decades. Its relationship with government power was, then, from its very earliest days, nothing like the cypherpunk vision of a new world with new roles, and no role for government.

Then there's the physical infrastructure that emerged, which, by the 1990s, the rapidly growing network relied upon. This is no cloud, no new world, no new means of communication. While its protocols might have been different and much more open than the heavily regulated and closed telephony networks of the 1970s and 1980s, the physical infrastructure is not fundamentally all that different.

That means that the internet's network of networks relies on the phone lines and the fibre-optic cables that powered its predecessors and ostensible rivals – though whether cable television or phone networks now count as rivals to the internet is questionable – in a highly regulated world. From long before most of us cared about the internet, it was mired in regulatory battles – and where there are regulatory power battles, there is the potential for power grabs, and for profits.

The new, online world built from the networks these cables facilitated was hardly unencumbered from the power players of the old world, though. When John Perry Barlow presented his declaration of the independence of cyberspace in 1996, he already knew it was an aspiration rather than a reality (much like the USA's own declaration of independence when it was first signed). How could he not, given he had co-founded EFF six years previously to fight government seizure of online communications?

The internet was born as a network between a few trusted individuals, with security largely unnecessary – an afterthought at best, and entirely absent even more often. That also meant privacy was barely there, which made mass interception of communications possible in a way it had never been before. When this was coupled with technological advances that made it ever easier to read and analyse that material without recourse to human workers, a cycle that could feed itself was begun.

This potential for increased government power was accelerated markedly with the birth of programmatic advertising, and the rapidly established norm that every site on the internet would obsessively track its users across the internet as an essential part of its business model.

This advertising model emerged independently of government – this did not require some nefarious conspiracy or collaboration between the two – but has served to replace the military-industrial complex with a military-informational complex,[2] where the needs of advertising, now one of the world's most important and lucrative sectors, fuels and services the needs of government.

Accelerating this growth was a surfeit of venture capital money fuelling the rise of dotcoms – encouraging them to pursue huge global scale over revenue, pushing them towards the ad model and helping to make sure the massive returns of the successful companies were concentrated in the hands of people who already had considerable personal wealth, as well as the institutional investors (universities, pension funds and similar) who had already enjoyed significant clout in the pre-internet world.

The financial crash served only to fuel this land-grab. Because central banks were determined to boost their economies and avoid a repeat of the huge economic depression of the early 1930s, they cut their interest rates as close as possible to zero – and then put hundreds of billions of their own cheap credit onto the market.

That meant there was no shortage of money chasing every possible opportunity, and with a generation of Silicon Valley firms growing up – the eBays and the PayPals of the world, the generation before the social internet – and achieving huge valuations, technology was an obvious sector in which to invest in a world which in some ways had more cash floating around than there were things in which to invest it.

That meant the incentives to go with the crowd, and follow the venture capital model, were all the higher – but also that most of the potential upside of the tech bubble was taken by the people at this phase, able to get early access as angel and seed investors, and lock up the later rounds, leaving even the relatively better-off members of the public who trade shares only able to take a stake at a much, much later stage, when most of the potential profits had already been taken.

All of this was allowed to happen by what must surely be assumed to be wilful blindness on behalf of the world's regulators and lawmakers. If two bricks-and-mortar retail stores want to merge, they face extensive regulatory oversight and analysis into whether that can be allowed.

When two of the UK's supermarket chains, Sainsbury's and Asda (owned by Walmart) wanted to merge in 2018, regulators all but stopped it – even in an era where both faced extensive online rivalry – for fears of loss of competition.[3] In the US, any owner of local newspapers or local television stations faced huge and serious scrutiny over any further acquisitions, and strict caps over how much they could own.

CONCLUSION

At the same time as the old world faced that level of scrutiny (itself often argued to be insufficient), Facebook was allowed to buy up WhatsApp, then a fast-growing messaging app and potential rival to its own services. Facebook had seen how rapidly the app's usage was increasing outside of the USA – and that high use of WhatsApp was correlated to spending less time with Facebook's apps – thanks to a third-party analytics app.

Facebook not only made the move to buy WhatsApp for a jaw-dropping $19 billion,[4] but it bought the analytics app that had given it the edge in spotting and quashing a potential rival, too. And no one was there to stop it, or even to question it. No one ever is.

THIS HAS ALL happened because we haven't been paying enough attention.

That's a problem that should be familiar to us by now: it works as a good explanation for the financial crash of 2008 and beyond, too – and the parallels are many. In the run-up to the financial crisis, there was a global property bubble. There was lots of cheap money, loans were easy to come by – even for people with low incomes, or no regular salary to speak of – and markets were booming.

And none of us asked the awkward questions as to why this was happening, and why house prices were going up far faster than salaries. There was some talk of, and coverage of, complex financial engineering – but this was dismissed as complicated and uninteresting. Who cares what a collateralised debt obligation or a synthetic position is anyway? The people who do the maths know how this stuff works, there are smart people running the banks, and the regulators seem happy enough with what's going on – and everyone's better off. Why worry?

This is what we do with the internet. Just as complicated financial jargon is enough to make most people's eyes glaze over, hearing about technical details of network architecture is very few people's idea of fun. That sense of complexity, and our aversion to it, allows powerful people to make decisions without too much attention being paid and without any awkward questions.

As Brian O'Kelley demonstrated, the fundamentals of the online ad world – notoriously one of the most complex enterprises going – can be explained in something very like human terms, and its inherent problems brought to light. So too can much of the rest. We need to learn to beware when people try to tell us not to worry about understanding detail.

That's because it's the systems we build, not the occasional panto villain, that cause disasters on a large scale. When things go wrong, it's our instinct to look for a bad guy, and to pin everything on them. In the UK, it was easy to target the Royal Bank of Scotland boss Sir Fred Goodwin – or 'Fred the Shred' – as the face of the financial crisis, the villain of the piece.[5]

Goodwin was hardly blameless: he'd spent years at the helm of a bank that had run a huge loan book, and relentlessly and aggressively expanded, and which eventually needed nationalisation to prevent the collapse of the financial system. The mockery he faced in the newspapers and the loss of his knighthood were minimal punishments over which few would shed tears.

In the wake of various privacy scandals at Facebook – among a relentless wave of bad PR over extremism, its corporate culture, censorship, and more – there's no shortage of people who would like to see its CEO Mark Zuckerberg similarly humbled.

That's not intrinsically wrong: the people at the top of the pyramid rarely face anything like the same kinds of consequences for their actions that the rest of us do. But tarring and feathering the odd executive won't change the system. We need to think bigger than that.

CONCLUSION

We need to become systems thinkers. We can't think about tackling Mark Zuckerberg, or even tackling Facebook, or social networking. The physical architecture of the internet is a network of networks.

The power base it enables is similarly interconnected – a new model for financing businesses, a new model for how they generate profit, and a new model of connectedness and transparency. Despite them feeling remote even to the people who built them, those systems were built by people, and so can be harnessed by them too – just as was done in the industrial era.

If we look at the systems which distribute power and money in the internet era, one fact is glaring: the winners are overwhelmingly white, overwhelmingly male, and overwhelmingly from the kind of background that was doing pretty much fine before the internet, too.

This explains some of the internet's blind spots, its cultural insensitivities, perhaps even why harassment and threats were so low down the agenda when the social internet companies were built. It's also not random chance: once the internet became the obvious forum for wealth and for fame, the world's existing power players were obviously going to move in on it – and they did.

The internet makes the pace of life faster. It makes physical distance largely irrelevant. It makes information far easier to find. But it doesn't change much else beyond that – and so in some ways all it does is help us repeat our mistakes, only faster than ever before.

Through this prism we have good reasons for concern about how the internet's expansion is working. Perhaps the ultimate example of this is Free Basics, an initiative by Facebook to expand internet access in less developed countries – by offering access to limited services from selected websites with no data charges.

Unsurprisingly, one of the sites that Free Basics prioritises is … Facebook. Which means that the expansion of the internet – viewed in the West as a utility, an increasingly essential service[6] – is principally in the hands of a private Western company, rather than the governments or other local agencies (though these have some involvement).

Research on the project in six of the countries in which it operates – Colombia, Ghana, Kenya, Mexico, Pakistan and the Philippines – found it was harvesting data in large quantities, serving as a launch pad for private companies and the services they offered, and in the process privileging US companies who would co-fund the scheme over potential local services or competitors.

The service also clearly violates the core tenets of net neutrality – the second a user tries to access services and information on the open internet, which is not specifically in the Free Basics programme, they are faced with a demand to pay for a data plan if they want to actually see that content. Not all data is treated equal.

The result is a state of being which can reasonably be described as a form of 'digital colonialism', an East India Company 2.0, once again sweeping the world, this time in the name of progress and of good intentions.[7]

This startling similarity should serve to knock us out of any kind of idea that the internet disrupts the top of established power structures. While it may serve as a technological shock which undermines the power of trade unions, of small retail stores and of all sorts of other workers across the economy – taxi drivers, warehouse workers and more – online power structures mirror almost exactly the offline power structures which preceded them.

TIM WU, THE Columbia Law School professor who coined the term 'net neutrality', certainly sees the parallels between the first Gilded Age, in the first decades of the twentieth century, and the internet era – or 'the new gilded age'. That first technological change had unquestionable upsides: it let us produce more goods, more efficiently and a lot more quickly than before.

In the long run, that made goods more affordable and helped garner – in some countries at least – the most rapid increase in living standards and wealth in human history. But spreading the benefits of the new technology did not happen automatically – and no entirely equitable spread ever happened. And in the immediate aftermath, people were told to just live with the negative effects that came along with technological change.

Writing in *The Curse of Bigness* of a J.P. Morgan project to unite the New Haven Railroad into a single service, Wu notes:

New Haven had, in fact, been based on a house of cards. As with many mega-mergers, organizational chaos soon followed the consolidation. Morgan's aggressive firing of workers and other cost-cutting measures were necessary to generate returns promised to shareholders, but they led to wrecks, derailments, and delays.

There were 24 deaths and 105 injuries in 1911 alone.

Even against that grim backdrop of the human toll of progress, Morgan was scathing of any would-be opponents. Of the trust-busting lawyer (and soon-to-be Supreme Court justice) Louis Brandeis's criticism of the New Haven project, Morgan simply said 'yellow dogs will bark and snap at the wheels of progress as they have since the beginning of time'.

The parallels deepen for Wu: the tactics of the would-be monopolists of both eras are virtually identical – he says that the net neutrality debate is, in many ways, a rehashing of the tactics used by John D. Rockefeller as he sought to leverage the market power he wielded in the railway network – the communications and shipment infrastructure of its day – to gain power in other sectors.

> Rockefeller began by banding together with the other large refiners in Cleveland and Pittsburgh, and they collectively struck a deal with the major railroads that guaranteed lower rates for their shipments while fixing prices higher for anyone out of the club. This part of his strategy exactly reflects today's battles over Net Neutrality, for Rockefeller used the key economic network of his time (the railroads) to ensure a major disadvantage for his smaller rivals.

This scheme – and different iterations and variations of it – were eventually found to be illegal in the antitrust battles of the twentieth century, and yet an almost identical fight has become one of the centrepieces of the battle for the internet, with almost no one drawing attention to the precedent. That short-termism costs us time and costs us victories, especially as Wu argues the twenty-first century is barely any more subtle than the twentieth, when bribes were overt and collusion was openly agreed in actual cigar-smoke-filled rooms.

Of Facebook's purchase of WhatsApp, he writes:

> The $19 billion buyout – as suspicious as J.P. Morgan's bribe of Andrew Carnegie – somehow failed to raise any alarm. At the time, many were shocked by the price. But when one is agreeing to split a monopoly as lucrative as generalized social media, with over $50 billion in annual revenue, the price suddenly makes sense.
>
> In total, Facebook managed to string together 67 unchallenged acquisitions, which seems impressive, unless you consider that Amazon undertook 91 and Google got away with 214.

CONCLUSION

Perhaps unsurprisingly for an academic expert in competition law, Wu believes antitrust law forms part of the answer – calling for a return to the eras of big, dramatic cases which served to then bring not only the monopoly in the courtroom to heel, but also the others who would otherwise imitate its behaviour.

Looking at technology – and citing Facebook, Google and Amazon as examples – Wu concludes: 'If there is a sector more ripe for the reinvigoration of the big case tradition, I don't know it.'

Given competition law was the most visible tool that was eventually used to bring the first Gilded Age to heel, it's easy to turn to it as the first resort for this second time around. But there are reasons for caution, too.

One is simply that it's rarely a good strategy to try to fight the last war all over again. Riding cavalry into trenches and machine guns in the First World War was a disaster. Trying to use trenches at all during the Second World War, in turn, proved to be a terrible idea. And so it is with political battles – we shouldn't automatically assume that what worked last time will work this time.

Part of that is just avoiding an automatic assumption – but there are specific grounds too. One is that corporations now have a century's experience in fighting antitrust cases and watering down antitrust laws. In the US at least, the Supreme Court has a comfortable Republican majority for the foreseeable future.

Even in the EU, where antitrust law is widely seen as stronger, authorities can only move beyond fines if they can demonstrate the only viable solution to the monopoly problem is breaking a company up – a very high bar. And any legal challenge will rely on the public authority winning despite being drastically out-lawyered: the tech giants can outspend even the world's largest competition authorities.

Even with those barriers, competition law may prove an invaluable tool in holding the power of the tech elite in check, and making the system work for all of us. But it shouldn't necessarily be the only tool in our arsenal – just as it wasn't the first time.

Building trade union laws, health and safety policies, laws governing working hours and ages were part of harnessing the industrial era to work for everyone – at least in part. There wasn't just one problem, so there wasn't just one fix. People might not have had a grand plan when passing each of these pieces of legislation – but did they even need to?

What measures does the equivalent of that package of reforms look for to tackle the digital era? We should not, one tech advocate argues, expect definitive answers straight away – if we think about the scale of the change that the internet has brought upon us, in his view, we are still in the very earliest days of the internet.

That man is Professor Jeff Jarvis, a persistent tech optimist, director of the Tow-Knight centre for entrepeneurial journalism at City University New York, and an adviser to multiple technology companies. One of his key suggestions is that the internet is a reform akin to the invention of the Gutenberg press – the first press to popularise the use of movable type, and so the modern era of printing as we know it.

'I always take a very long-term view of this, that's my shtick, I'll admit,' Jarvis explains when I meet him in a Manhattan Starbucks. 'But movable type was invented in 1450, or developed in 1450, to give the Chinese credit, too. It took fifty years for the books to take the form we know, a century, according to Elizabeth Eisenstein [academic historian and author of *The Printing Press as an Agent of Change*], before the impact on society was fully felt, a century and a half before the self-evident invention of a newspaper came along.'

CONCLUSION

By Jarvis's reasoning, when it comes to the internet, then, if the web browser is the equivalent of movable type, we're still 120 years before someone even thinks of the newspaper – so it's far too early to look for what's working and what isn't.

'We're at 1474 right now in Gutenberg time. Martin Luther wasn't born yet. We don't know what this is yet. I argued this is very long term, that's why I'm not concerned about the oligopoly on the platforms because they have much more change ahead of us.'

It would be churlish to say Jarvis doesn't have a point here: if we had jumped every time a company looked as if it was about to dominate the internet, we could have stepped in to create laws to stifle AOL, or MySpace, or Microsoft. Who dominates the internet does seem to change every five to ten years.

On the other hand, it seems unfair to have to wait another 130 or so years until we're happy to assess what the fallout of the internet was. The world moves far faster now than it did in 1450.

FROM THIS TANGLE, can we find answers? I think so. One of the fundamental insights is the one raised by Egyptian activist and former Google product manager Wael Ghonim – we should see the internet as a tool, and nothing more. Not something with any built-in ideology, not something with any kind of inherent good or ill.

The big question with a tool is who controls it: we feel very differently seeing our relative with a hammer, hanging a picture, than we would seeing the same hammer in the hands of someone with a ski mask, running at our house's window. If the internet is a tool for creating wealth, creating networks and creating communication, it's currently in the hands of the elite.

That's much the same as the railways, the cotton mills and the other tools of industry at the turn of the twentieth century, which were firmly in the hands of the industrialists.

Rather than trying to tackle each individual company, or to try to solve every problem with one grand plan, we need to learn how to push lots of changes at once to improve different aspects of how the system works. As Amazon 'disrupts' jobs with its punishing warehouse conditions and non-existent job security – as Facebook and others do with moderators – we need to come up with new contracts and worker protections to counteract that.

As Google, Facebook, advertising networks and others build multi-billion-dollar businesses based on data, we need to work out how to treat personal data now it's so valuable. Given it's about us as citizens, as human beings, and it's often about deeply personal aspects of our lives, should it be so easy for companies to own? Could it be made more transferable? Could companies be required to share profits on it? Could we shift away from the data-driven online ad model, if it doesn't lead to better quality content, and it doesn't lead to better choices for us as consumers?

There is more we can do on tax, and how we get companies which span the planet to pay a fair share. We can require algorithms to be independently tested and vetted for systematic inequality or biases, whether based on race, class, gender, sexuality. We can demand more from the institutions which invest our pensions and other funds through venture capital.

Technology companies often coach us to expect one big fix. History tells us to look for lots of smaller ones, if we actually want sustainable change.

Step one is to make sure we learn how this stuff actually works, so we don't get bamboozled into inaction, as we did with finance. Step two is to treat the technology companies as just regular corporations – not something new, not something mission-driven, just regular companies that follow their usual incentives. Step three is to remember that the technology itself today actually is different, and so we shouldn't expect what worked yesterday still to work today or tomorrow.

We moved fast and we broke things, and we didn't act quickly enough to repair the damage as we did so, often because it worked out in the interests of the USA, its elite and its government. The rise of China's technology giants and the ebbing of the USA's unilateral dominance of the internet could mark a scary inflection point – but it can also be our spur to action.

Unless something drastically changes, China, with its very different norms and its very different priorities, will be the host of companies managing the next generation of the internet's architecture. That reduces the USA's built-in advantage, and creates a reason to build in better privacy protections, better security and less power to the companies and governments managing the networks.

We can see that change as a threat, or as an opportunity. The scale of what we need to do to make the internet work for us is daunting, but it is achievable – especially if we break it down into getting lots of small things done, rather than trying to rebuild the communications backbone of the world all in one go.

We know it can be done, because it's been done before. It's the next step of the technological revolution, and it's in our hands.

A NOTE ON CONTRIBUTORS

This book would have been impossible without the time and generosity of a number of people who made themselves available for interview, and allowed themselves to become representatives of different tribes who built the internet, made it like it is, or in some way contributed to what I, at least, would describe as the mess we're in today.

I hope those people like the book, and agree – at least in part – with its diagnosis of what's happening and the scale of the action needed to tackle it. But while I hope they will all find they have been quoted fairly and accurately, and their views at the time they spoke to me reflected on the topics they're talking about, the ideas in this book are mine and are my responsibility.

Some of the people featured are far more optimistic about the internet today, and its potential tomorrow, than I am. Some are gloomier. Each has their own idea, and many of them have their own Twitter feeds, blogs or even books setting those out. I urge you to seek them out if you'd like more views on where we are now.

All of which is to say: inclusion in this book is not an endorsement – especially as several chapters profile people unwilling to grant even the shortest of interviews or statements. So if there's any blame or backlash to the ideas or the issues raised herein, do, please, take them up with me, and not the people I've spoken to along the way.

ACKNOWLEDGEMENTS

This section can only open thanking all the people who gave generously of their time for interviews, whether on or off the record. That includes Albert Wenger, Ben Cos, Brian O'Kelley, Cindy Cohn, Emily Bell, Frank Eliason, Göran Marby, Jeff Greene, Jeff Jarvis – special thanks to him for his generosity with his contacts book – Jimmy Wales, John Borthwick, Steve Crocker, everyone at Symantec, Tom Daly, Tom Wheeler and Wael Ghonim. Bonus thanks to Brad White at ICANN for all his help, and Julia Powles for her wisdom.

From my perspective – and hopefully from theirs – this book's been a joy from a publishing side, thanks to great support from my agent Tracy Bohan at Wylie, and a great editing team at Bloomsbury in the shape of Alexis Kirschbaum, Jasmine Horsey, Katherine Fry and Lauren Whybrow.

Reporting a book like this involves a lot of travel on a tiny budget, so copious thanks are due to Amna Saleem, Elena Egawhary, Megan Carpentier, Laurence Dodds, Nicky Woolf and Tess McCormick for providing places for me to stay, report or write from – and often good company too – during the work on the book. Particular thanks are also due to Nick Hancock and his current fiancée for actually giving up their home permanently during the reporting of the book.

Several chapters of this book draw from previous reporting projects I've been lucky to have been part of. On WikiLeaks,

ACKNOWLEDGEMENTS

David Leigh and Luke Harding were a pleasure to work with and their book is a valuable reminder of the time. LSE's Charlie Beckett was a joy to co-write an academic book with on the era. As to those within WikiLeaks itself, the good ones know who they are, even if the world doesn't – and Chelsea Manning deserves to be a free woman.

I discovered the surprisingly strange world of ICANN thanks to a story idea from Merope Mills, and worked with Laurence Mathieu-Léger reporting the feature and the video, which was a joy.

Thanks are of course due to the extensive *Guardian* team reporting the Snowden documents, notably Glenn Greenwald, Ewen MacAskill, Spencer Ackerman, Julian Borger, Nick Hopkins and numerous others. Particular credit has to go to our steadfast editors Janine Gibson and Stuart Millar, and of course to the then editor-in-chief Alan Rusbridger. And Luke Harding once again should be noted as the one who got it all into a book at the time. But the bulk of the credit for some of the most important revelations of the modern internet era have to go to the source himself, Edward Snowden.

Credit and thanks are due to anyone working or who has worked at the organisations fighting for our online freedoms – the EFF, but also Open Rights Group, Privacy International, Liberty, the ACLU and others. They are in so many areas both our canary in the mine and our front-line fighters.

Finally, on a practical note, I'd like to thank lots of friends who've read parts of the manuscript, let me bounce ideas off them, listened to my panics when stuck, and more. These include Luke, Marie, Caroline, Holly, Louis, Jasper, Tom C, Tom P, David, Alastair, Alix and several of the people already listed, plus – inevitably – some I'll have forgotten.

And thanks, I suppose, to my cats for routinely sleeping on the keyboard as I wrote. I think I've managed to delete most of your input by now.

GLOSSARY

The internet world is one full of jargon, often technical and often confusing. This book doesn't expect you to know any of this when you begin reading, and tries to tackle and explain the alphabet soup of terms, but this serves to reference anything missing or which might come in helpful.

4G: short for '4th generation', this is the existing standard of high-speed internet – mainly for mobile devices – being rolled out across countries around the world.

5G: this is '5th generation', the much faster next era of wireless internet technology, which is expected to be competitive with wired internet for browsing speed. It is the subject of a briefing and trade war between China and the US, and the focus of concerns for the future of net neutrality.

ad exchange: the platform which manages one of the final stages of matching a user to an online ad, this arranges an instant online auction between advertisers based on what they know about the user.

angel investor: a relatively early-stage tech investor who will put in a sum, usually in the six-figure region, and who will take a considerable stake in a company and work to boost its profile.

ARPANET: this is the network that became the internet, a connection of US universities and other institutions, which eventually became defunct at the end of the 1980s. Named after ARPA/DARPA, the US government research agencies which initially funded it.

BGP: Border Gateway Protocol, a system devised on the back of a napkin which helps govern how traffic flows across the internet to this very day.

blockchain: a form of distributed, verifiable database that is typically used to power cryptocurrencies. Still in its infancy, there are hopes blockchain represents a chance to break the power held by existing database gatekeepers.

cookies: small text files left on your computer or phone by sites as you browse the internet. While they leave little information on your own device, they can be used remotely to track each time the cookie is seen and store much, much richer information.

CPM: short for cost per mille, this is the standard metric for valuing online ads, and is the amount the advertiser pays for each 1,000 views (or impressions) that an advert receives.

DARPA: short for the Defense Advanced Research Projects Agency, this is the US military's special research projects team – and was the first funder for the precursor to the internet.

DARPANET: see ARPANET.

data broker: a company – usually not a household name – that buys up commercially available data on millions of users and packages and sells it on to others. This is used for credit rating and similar purposes, but also used to 'enrich' data in online advertising, to learn more by joining data together, often without users' knowledge.

DDoS: short for distributed denial of service, this is a form of attack against a website or online service that involves thousands of computers – usually compromised without their users' knowledge – overloading a site with an impossible flood of requests. A common and crude form of online attack.

dial-up: a common early means of connecting to the internet via standard telephone cables. A modem would convert the digital signals to analogue and send them as beeps via the phone lines. This was much slower than modern connections, and phone calls would disconnect the internet.

DMP: short for data management platform, these companies organise data for ad targeters to use – sometimes adding to it with data from a data broker – and passing it to a DSP to give to an ad exchange to enable bidding for ads to happen.

DNS: the Domain Name System, a set of rules that govern which online addresses (e.g. 'google.com') match to which IP addresses, and how these are looked up and distributed.

DSP: short for demand side platform, part of the programmatic advertising process that gives information on the kind of user (or even individual users, such as lists of existing customers) advertisers would like to target online to ad exchanges.

encryption: the key standard of online security, based on the fact it's easy to generate large numbers from large prime numbers, but very hard to decode this the other way. This is what lets data be protected for two-way communication, protecting our financial information, personal data and even our critical infrastructure.

FCC: the Federal Communications Commission, a powerful US regulator set up in the first half of the twentieth century with wide-ranging powers over phone, radio, broadcast and the internet.

GCHQ: originally an initialism of Government Communications Headquarters, this is the UK's signals intelligence agency, responsible for interception and intelligence across electronic communications, while also having responsibility for UK online security.

ICANN: short for the Internet Corporation for Assigned Names and Numbers, ICANN is the not-for-profit body in charge of managing DNS.

IMP: short for Interface Message Processor, this was a precursor to a router which enabled communications between computers across ARPANET.

internet: originally a shorthand for inter-network, the internet is essentially a network of networks, letting separate (and often secure) systems communicate globally.

IP: short for Internet Protocol (and properly referred to as an IP address), this is the system for assigning a unique number for each node on the internet network. These look like a string of random numbers (mine is currently 82.20.204.12), and are made to correspond to online addresses via DNS.

IPO: short for initial public offering, this is the most common way companies launch on public listings, such as the Dow, NASDAQ or FTSE – selling some of their shares and taking a publicly listed share price. This is how VCs 'exit' a company and recoup their investment.

ISP: short for internet service provider, the company responsible for actually connecting you to the internet, for which you, the customer, pay a monthly fee. ISPs are usually also cable or telecoms companies.

net neutrality: a key debate about the future of the internet, the idea of 'net neutrality' is that all data travelling across the internet is treated the same – that a packet is a packet, whether it's Netflix video, email or a website.

network: a collection of computing devices connected to each other so they can communicate and transfer data. These can be generalised or very specific (such as for specialist airline systems and so on). They pre-date ARPANET.

network slicing: a capability of 5G that lets traffic of different types be handled differently, which can let the network work more efficiently – but which also raises net neutrality fears among critics.

GLOSSARY

NSA: the National Security Agency, the USA's signals (electronic communications) intelligence agency. A far better-funded equivalent to GCHQ.

packets: one of the key innovations which DARPA wanted to check when it agreed to fund ARPANET, and still a core internet technology. Anything sent via the internet is broken up into small 'packets' of data, each of which can take its own route to the destination, where they are reassembled. A key principle of the internet is that all packets are treated the same.

protocol: the term for the rules and procedures that govern how particular types of data transmission are handled. 'HTTP', or 'HyperText Transfer Protocol', governs how web traffic works; 'SMTP', or 'Simple Mail Transfer Protocol', handles email; and so on.

RFC: short for Request For Comment, which despite the unassuming name is how new core protocols for how the internet functions are introduced and communicated.

router: a device that routes traffic across different networks, effectively enabling the function of the internet. The (usually wireless) box in your house which enables your internet is a router.

server: a term for a computer connected to the internet that's intended to serve some form of content – a web server delivers web content, email servers handle emails, and so on. These are typically specialist high-end machines kept in data centres and professionally managed.

SSP: short for supply side platform, this is the other side of the online ad auction process, which passes on information to ad exchanges to allow the sale of ad space.

TCP: short for transmission control protocol, this is one of the key protocols governing how data flows over the internet, introduced alongside IP in its early days.

venture capital/VC: the financial model (and financial backer) of most of the internet, venture capital is a particular subset of private equity which invests in tech firms, hoping for returns of ten times or more.

World Wide Web: the web is the most obvious and visible bit of the internet to most of us, conceived in 1989 by Tim Berners-Lee, and is the system by which websites are delivered to browsers such as Chrome, Firefox or Safari.

FURTHER READING

The following serve as a selected bibliography of the books used in the research of this book, as well as a few not cited herein but which offer good background or further reading on some of the topics covered. This isn't comprehensive – it doesn't include books or papers cited in passing, but these are included in the endnotes.

Anderson, C., *The Long Tail: Why the Future of Business Is Selling Less of More*, Hachette Books, 2008.

Bamford, J., *The Shadow Factory: The Ultra-Secret NSA from 9/11 to the Eavesdropping on America*, Anchor, 2009.

Bartlett, J., *People Vs Tech*, Ebury Press, 2018.

Beckett, C., and Ball, J., *Wikileaks: News in the Networked Era*, Polity, 2012.

Blum, A., *Tubes*, Viking, 2019.

Greenwald, G., *No Place to Hide: Edward Snowden, the NSA and the Surveillance State*, Penguin UK, 2015.

Harding, L., *The Snowden Files*, Guardian Faber Publishing, 2016.

Leigh, D., *Wikileaks: Inside Julian Assange's War on Secrecy*, Guardian Books, 2010.

Miller, C., *The Death of the Gods: The New Global Power Grab*, Windmill Books, 2019.

Susskind, J., *Future Politics: Living Together in a World Transformed by Tech*, Oxford University Press, 2018.

Wu, T., *The Curse of Bigness: Antitrust in the New Gilded Age*, Columbia Global Reports, 2018.

Zittrain, J., *The Future of the Internet – And How to Stop It* (s.n.), Yale University Press, 2009.

Zuboff, S., *The Age of Surveillance Capitalism: The Fight for the Future at the New Frontier of Power*, Profile Books Ltd, 2019.

NOTES

INTRODUCTION

1   This analysis takes some inspiration and reasoning from Tim Wu's *The Curse of Bigness*, cited at greater length in the conclusion.

2   https://www.washingtonpost.com/news/wonk/wp/2017/12/06/the-richest-1-percent-now-owns-more-of-the-countrys-wealth-than-at-any-time-in-the-past-50-years/?noredirect=on&utm_term=.e7adba67bfe6

3   https://www.bbc.co.uk/news/business-42745853

1 THE ARCHITECTS

1   US broadband speed taken from http://fortune.com/2017/06/02/internet-speed-akamai-survey/

2   The narrative of the first internet message is taken from this (charming and very readable) transcript: https://archive.icann.org/meetings/losangeles2014/en/schedule/mon-crocker-kleinrock/transcript-crocker-kleinrock-13oct14-en.pdf

3   https://www.internethalloffame.org//inductees/steve-crocker

4   https://ai.google/research/people/author32412

5   Wired have a great feature with much more detail on 'the mother of all demos' here: https://www.wired.com/2010/12/1209computer-mouse-mother-of-all-demos/

6   This was the recollection of Bob Taylor, who secured the funding (https://www.computer.org/csdl/magazine/an/2011/03/man2011030004/13rRUxly9fL), but was disputed by Charles

Herzfeld, who said he had agreed the funding, but had taken more than twenty minutes' persuasion (https://www.wired.com/2012/08/herzfeld/).

7 Full video and transcript: http://opentranscripts.org/transcript/steve-crocker-internet-hall-fame-2012-profile/

8 This is also from Kleinrock's 2014 transcript: https://archive.icann.org/meetings/losangeles2014/en/schedule/mon-crocker-kleinrock/transcript-crocker-kleinrock-13oct14-en.pdf

9 https://www.ietf.org/rfc/rfc0675.txt

10 ARPANET had operated as a packet switching network from its inception – TCP is just a specific implantation of the concept, and the one which came to be the standard.

11 This paragraph borrows key dates from https://www.webfx.com/blog/web-design/the-history-of-the-internet-in-a-nutshell/

12 Everything from Steve Lukasik comes from his paper 'Why the ARPANET Was Built', published online here: https://www.academia.edu/34728504/WHY_THE_ARPANET_WAS_BUILT

13 This is from the Crocker/Kleinrock discussion.

14 https://webfoundation.org/about/vision/history-of-the-web/

15 These are sourced to the Internet Services Consortium, but most easily viewed on Wikipedia https://en.wikipedia.org/wiki/Global_Internet_usage

16 https://www.bbc.co.uk/news/technology-32884867

17 https://www.statista.com/statistics/471264/iot-number-of-connected-devices-worldwide/

18 This stat comes from TeleGeography (https://www2.telegeography.com/submarine-cable-faqs-frequently-asked-questions) – their map of the main undersea internet cables is well worth a look: https://www.submarinecablemap.com/

2 THE CABLE GUYS

1 http://www.washingtonpost.com/wp-dyn/content/article/2007/10/17/AR2007101702359.html?hpid=artslot

2 All of Eliason's comments in this chapter are from an interview with the author.

3 Ofcom data is available here: https://www.ofcom.org.uk/__data/assets/pdf_file/0022/145525/comparing-service-quality-2018.pdf

NOTES

4   Calculated from ARPU (average revenue per internet user), sourced here: https://www.nscreenmedia.com/comcast/

5   This tale is contained within this Wired profile of Brian Roberts and Comcast: https://web.archive.org/web/20130107032943/http://www.wired.com/techbiz/people/magazine/17-02/mf_brianroberts?currentPage=all

6   To replicate this on Mac – though your results will be different – open Terminal, and type 'traceroute www.twitter.com' and wait a few minutes, and you'll have gobbledegook of your very own.

7   IPs geolocated through https://iplocation.com, correct as at February 2019.

8   Really: https://www.wired.co.uk/article/shark-cables

9   https://arstechnica.com/information-technology/2014/07/how-comcast-became-a-powerful-and-controversial-part-of-the-internet-backbone/

10 https://www.trustedreviews.com/news/what-is-5g-vs-4g-2911748

11 It's worth noting Eliason said he thought the industry had since got better – to the point he'd consider working there again. 'I'm not certain they would take me but …' he added.

12 https://motherboard.vice.com/en_us/article/bjdjd4/100-million-americans-only-have-one-isp-option-internet-broadband-net-neutrality

13 https://www.opensecrets.org/lobby/indusclient.php?id=B09&year=a

14 https://www.opensecrets.org/lobby/indusclient.php?id=B13&year=2018

15 There's a good summary of this structure here: https://www.cnbc.com/2018/03/20/shareholders-wont-force-zuckerbergs-hand-in-facebook-management.html

16 Yes, really: https://bgr.com/2018/06/13/comcast-ceo-brian-roberts-customer-satisfaction/

3 THE CUSTODIANS

1   This is written up at length as a feature in the *Guardian*'s Saturday magazine, available online here: https://www.theguardian.com/technology/2014/feb/28/seven-people-keys-worldwide-internet-security-web

2   This and the following information is taken from the original RFC for DNS, online here: https://www.ietf.org/rfc/rfc1034.txt

3 https://www.fireeye.com/blog/threat-research/2019/01/global-dns-hijacking-campaign-dns-record-manipulation-at-scale.html

4 Its founding chair was angel investor Esther Dyson, one of the rare cases in which a woman took a leading role in an internet institution. She served as chair from 1998 to 2000.

5 https://www.theguardian.com/technology/2016/mar/14/icann-internet-control-domain-names-iana

6 https://www.theguardian.com/technology/2016/oct/26/ddos-attack-dyn-mirai-botnet

7 https://www.theregister.co.uk/2018/02/12/icann_corp_home_mail_gtlds/

8 This depends who you ask: BGP is commonly referred to as both the 'two napkin' and the 'three napkin' protocol – but those closest to its invention cite the latter, so we have gone with that: https://www.washingtonpost.com/sf/business/2015/05/31/net-of-insecurity-part-2/?utm_term=.07bae5cfc2d9

9 https://www.computerhistory.org/atchm/the-two-napkin-protocol/

10 This is a close approximation but not exact – it can tell you if a road is closed or not, but it can't give you any sense of how much traffic there is going to be. So like a not-very-good satnav.

11 https://tools.ietf.org/html/rfc1105

12 You can take a look at the live stats here: https://www.fastly.com/

13 https://dyn.com/blog/pakistan-hijacks-youtube-1/

14 https://arstechnica.com/information-technology/2018/11/major-bgp-mishap-takes-down-google-as-traffic-improperly-travels-to-china/

15 https://bgpmon.net/popular-destinations-rerouted-to-russia/

16 https://arstechnica.com/information-technology/2018/04/suspicious-event-hijacks-amazon-traffic-for-2-hours-steals-cryptocurrency/

17 https://www.cyberscoop.com/telegram-iran-bgp-hijacking/

18 https://www.industryweek.com/economy/infrastructure-crumbles-so-does-us-manufacturing

19 https://www2.deloitte.com/insights/us/en/economy/issues-by-the-numbers/us-aging-water-infrastructure-investment-opportunities.html

20 https://edition.cnn.com/2016/03/04/us/flint-water-crisis-fast-facts/index.html

21 https://www.theregister.co.uk/2018/02/06/us_broadband_
fcc_report/

4 THE MONEY MEN

1 Yes, the company uses a small 'b' and we've decided to stick to it,
except at the start of sentences.

2 https://techcrunch.com/2016/05/20/twitter-and-betaworks-
are-teaming-up-in-a-new-fund/

3 https://betaworksventures.com/our-companies

4 https://www.bizjournals.com/newyork/blog/techflash/2015/03/
playdots-betaworks-mobile-video-game-twodots.html

5 https://www.businessinsider.com.au/fotolog-still-g-2007-9

6 The analysis that follows is from a variety of sources and interviews,
but a helpful guide (and the rough ranges for round sizes used
here) can be found at https://support.crunchbase.com/hc/en-us/
articles/115010458467-Glossary-of-Funding-Types

7 Deliveroo raised $70 million as its Series C: https://techcrunch.
com/2015/07/27/series-c-delivered/

8 Uber, meanwhile, raised more than $300 million: https://
techcrunch.com/2013/08/22/google-ventures-puts-
258m-into-uber-its-largest-deal-ever/

9 This is $400,000 post-money, to be technical, but doesn't really
matter for this example.

10 https://adage.com/article/digital/sean-parker-worries-
facebook-rotting-children-s-brains/311238/

11 This argument is well evidenced here: https://www.buzzfeednews.
com/article/charliewarzel/why-facebook-bought-whatsapp

12 This and the next few sentences on USV are taken from this 2017
blogpost: https://avc.com/2017/10/our-model/

13 https://www.usv.com/about/albert-wenger

14 If you're spotting a lot of overlap with betaworks … welcome to
big tech.

15 I believe the event referred to here is the Coronation of George V in
June 1911, rather than the funeral of his predecessor.

5 THE AD MEN

1 https://www.wsj.com/articles/at-t-to-acquire-digital-ad-firm-
appnexus-for-1-6-billion-1529929278?mod=article_inline

NOTES

2 https://www.cnbc.com/2019/02/04/alphabet-earnings-q4-2018.html

3 https://s21.q4cdn.com/399680738/files/doc_financials/2018/Q4/Q4-2018-Earnings-Release.pdf

4 https://www.digitalcommerce360.com/article/amazon-sales/

5 This is very standard phrasing, but in this instance was taken from the *Washington Post* website.

6 These figures were collected in February 2019, browsing from the UK, using the Chrome extension Ghostery.

7 This is a summary of an extended analysis of what happens as you browse the internet, which I first published with HuffPost UK: https://www.huffingtonpost.co.uk/entry/what-happens-when-you-click_uk_5bb60455e4b028e1fe3b43a3

8 https://www.zergnet.com/0/3745780/1/0/2499551/1/ (working as at February 2019)

9 https://www.zergnet.com/0/3735076/1/0/2499551/2/ (working as at February 2019)

10 https://www.zergnet.com/0/3767013/1/0/2499551/11/ (working as at February 2019)

11 https://www.pinknews.co.uk/pagicle/43-celebrities-you-didnt-know-were-gay-bisexual-or-lesbian-ellen

12 If you have never encountered this *Avenue Q* song, you should. It's on YouTube here: https://www.youtube.com/watch?v=zBDCq6Q8k2E

13 At the time of writing, the research paper had not yet been formally published, but had been circulated (including to the author) as a preliminary draft under the working title 'Tracking Technologies and Publishers Revenues: An Empirical Analysis'.

14 http://nymag.com/intelligencer/2018/12/how-much-of-the-internet-is-fake.html

15 If you access it from an EU country, anyway.

6 THE CYBER WARRIORS

1 The eventual reporting team on this story was Ewen MacAskill, Julian Borger, Nick Hopkins, Nick Davies and me – David Leigh did not take a byline. The published story is here: https://www.theguardian.com/uk/2013/jun/21/gchq-cables-secret-world-communications-nsa

NOTES

2   The background of the story behind the Snowden revelations is my personal recollection, drawn from first-hand knowledge and conversations with those present at the time – though memory is, of course, fallible. Sources to specific stories, references and documents are credited separately. For a full accounting of the Snowden tale, take a look at Luke Harding's or Glenn Greenwald's books on the period.

3   It worked out: reader, she hired me.

4   https://foreignpolicy.com/2013/09/09/the-cowboy-of-the-nsa/

5   The *Washington Post* notes Alexander did not design this command room himself, but does note he was a fan of it: https://www.washingtonpost.com/blogs/in-the-loop/wp/2013/09/16/nsa-director-inherited-star-trek-digs/?noredirect=on&utm_term=.4bed42c574b7

6   This explanation is taken from the earlier cited Tempora story, from https://www.theguardian.com/uk/2013/jun/21/gchq-mastering-the-internet, and from my own reporting notes from that time.

7   The full show can be viewed on YouTube here: https://www.youtube.com/watch?v=XEVlyP4_11M

8   Optic Nerve was first disclosed in a 2014 Snowden story, reported with Spencer Ackerman: https://www.theguardian.com/world/2014/feb/27/gchq-nsa-webcam-images-internet-yahoo

9   https://www.ft.com/content/93fe2e28-d83c-11e2-b4a4-00144feab7de

10   https://www.propublica.org/article/claim-on-attacks-thwarted-by-nsa-spreads-despite-lack-of-evidence

11   https://www.npr.org/2018/12/28/677414459/in-chinas-push-for-high-tech-hackers-target-cutting-edge-u-s-firms?t=1550197762515

12   To learn more about Stuxnet, and the massive cyber-programme it was part of, the best source is Alex Gibney's documentary *Zero Days*. I reported some of its revelations, with independent corroboration, here: https://www.buzzfeednews.com/article/jamesball/us-hacked-into-irans-critical-civilian-infrastructure-for-ma

13   https://www.thebureauinvestigates.com/stories/2018-09-13/bureau-wins-case-to-defend-press-freedom-at-the-european-court-of-human-rights

14   https://www.theguardian.com/world/2013/oct/24/nsa-surveillance-world-leaders-calls

15 As with other stories, they did agree to redact certain specific details (for example, particular models of software, or company names, when specific reasons were given).

16 The *Guardian* version of this story can be viewed here: https://www.theguardian.com/world/2013/sep/05/nsa-gchq-encryption-codes-security

17 This was helpfully tweeted by the BBC's technology editor, Rory Cellan-Jones: https://twitter.com/ruskin147/status/1096327971131088896/photo/1

18 The following account of WannaCry is based on interviews with the Symantec staff in the chapter, my own reporting from the time (https://www.buzzfeed.com/jamesball/heres-why-its-unlikely-the-nhs-was-deliberately-targeted-in, https://www.buzzfeed.com/jamesball/gchq-is-facing-questions-over-last-weeks-ransomware-attack, https://www.buzzfeed.com/jamesball/a-highly-critical-report-says-the-nhs-was-hit-by-the), and some details from this later *Washington Post* report: https://www.washingtonpost.com/world/national-security/us-set-to-declare-north-korea-carried-out-massive-wannacry-cyber-attack/2017/12/18/509deb1c-e446-11e7-a65d-1acofd7fo97e_story.html?utm_term=.5616081ea532

19 https://www.theregister.co.uk/2019/02/14/marcus_hutchins_evidence/

20 https://techcrunch.com/2018/01/09/chinas-kunlun-completes-full-buyout-of-grindr/

21 https://techcrunch.com/2019/02/11/reddit-300-million/

22 https://bpr.berkeley.edu/2018/02/09/a-call-for-caution-indias-aadhaar/

23 This is, as this article explains, a simplification – but about as close as can be explained in one sentence: https://www.wired.co.uk/article/china-social-credit-system-explained

7 THE RULEMAKERS

1 You can watch it, if you'd like, here (but I recommend giving it a miss): https://dailycaller.com/2017/12/13/ajit-pai-wants-you-to-know-you-can-still-harlem-shake-after-net-neutrality-video/

2 https://www.salon.com/2017/08/21/the-daily-caller-has-a-white-nationalist-problem_partner/

NOTES

3 https://www.theatlantic.com/politics/archive/2018/09/a-daily-caller-editor-wrote-for-an-alt-right-website-using-a-pseudonym/569335/

4 https://www.theguardian.com/us-news/2016/dec/05/washington-pizza-child-sex-ring-fake-news-man-charged

5 You can watch it here (but once again, I'd recommend not): https://www.youtube.com/watch?v=KFx34mEnOig

6 https://c-7npsfqifvtox24epdtx2egddx2ehpw.goo.cnet.com/goo/3_c-7x78x78x78.dofu.dpn_/c-7NPSFQIFVTox24iuuqtx3ax2fx2fepdt.gdd.hpwx2fqvcmjdx2fbuubdinfoutx2fGDD-29-267B3.qeg_$/$/$/$?i10c.ua=1&i10c.dv=17

7 https://www.nytimes.com/2017/05/01/business/dealbook/tv-station-owners-rush-to-seize-on-relaxed-fcc-rules.html

8 https://www.nytimes.com/2017/11/16/business/media/fcc-local-tv.html

9 https://www.nytimes.com/2018/04/02/business/media/sinclair-news-anchors-script.html

10 There's a good discussion of net neutrality as a free speech issue here: https://motherboard.vice.com/en_us/article/kbye4z/heres-why-net-neutrality-is-essential-in-trumps-america

11 https://gizmodo.com/ajit-pai-thinks-youre-stupid-enough-to-buy-this-crap-1821277398

12 https://www.wired.com/2017/03/ex-fcc-boss-gut-net-neutrality-gut-internet-freedom/

13 https://motherboard.vice.com/en_us/article/xygmbk/fcc-chairman-tom-wheeler-net-neutrality-champion-says-hell-step-down

14 http://time.com/4770205/john-oliver-fcc-net-neutrality/

15 https://www.cnet.com/news/fccs-net-neutrality-ddos-story-falls-apart-ajit-pai-blames-previous-admin/; https://www.kitguru.net/tech-news/featured-tech-news/damien-cox/ajit-pai-was-aware-that-fcc-ddos-attack-was-a-lie-in-january-but-reportedly-couldnt-say/

16 https://www.cnet.com/news/eric-schneiderman-new-york-attorney-general-2-million-net-neutrality-comments-were-fake/

17 https://www.techdirt.com/articles/20181204/07033241154/fcc-commissioner-accuses-her-own-agency-net-neutrality-cover-up.shtml

18 https://c-7npsfqifvtox24epdtx2egddx2ehpw.goo.cnet.com/
goo/3_c-7x78x78x78.dofu.dpn_/c-7NPSFQIFVTox24iuuqtx3ax
2fx2fepdt.gdd.hpwx2fqvcmjdx2fbuubdinfoutx2fGDD-29-267B3.
qeg_$/$/$/$?i1oc.ua=1&i1oc.dv=17

19 https://www.techdirt.com/articles/20181207/08072441177/
contrary-to-media-claims-theres-no-evidence-russia-was-behind-
fake-net-neutrality-comments.shtml

20 http://www.publicconsultation.org/wp-content/uploads/2017/
12/Net_Neutrality_Quaire_121217.pdf

21 https://gizmodo.com/only-1-in-5-republicans-want-the-fcc-to-gut-
net-neutral-1821231973

22 This is from our conversation, but Tom Wheeler's book on this
should be out by the time you read this. It's *From Gutenberg to
Google: The History of our Future, The Brookings Instiution, 2019.*

23 http://www.analysysmason.com/About-Us/News/Newsletter/
net-neutrality-rules-in-europe-jul17/

24 Part one: https://twitter.com/realDonaldTrump/status/
1098581869233344512, part two: https://twitter.com/
realDonaldTrump/status/1098583029713420288

25 There is a good explainer on what's behind Trump's tweet here:
https://www.washingtonpost.com/news/powerpost/paloma/the-
cybersecurity-202/2019/02/25/the-cybersecurity-202-on-huawei-
policy-it-s-trump-vs-the-trump-administration/5c72e0731b326b718
58c6c23/?utm_term=.77032a06a277

26 https://www.cnet.com/news/huawei-reportedly-sides-with-trump-
on-5g-us-is-lagging-behind/

8 THE RESISTANCE

1 https://www.nytimes.com/2004/07/18/us/letter-from-san-
francisco-a-beautiful-promenade-turns-ugly-and-a-city-blushes.html

2 There's a lot to nerd out on about Apple's campus, and if you'd like
to do so, this Wired piece on it is excellent: https://www.wired.
com/2017/05/apple-park-new-silicon-valley-campus/

3 https://www.adweek.com/digital/facebooks-menlo-park-campus-
now-has-a-new-frank-gehry-designed-building/

4 https://www.fastcompany.com/3068889/googles-newly-approved-
hq-are-the-perfect-metaphor-for-silicon-valley

5 https://www.theguardian.com/technology/2017/jun/01/google-
submits-plans-million-sq-ft-london-hq-construction-kings-cross

NOTES

6 https://www.eff.org/about/staff

7 $11 million in 2016–17, as its audited accounts show, but that has increased, as Cohn told me, and see https://www.eff.org/document/2016-2017-audited-financial-statement

8 https://www.nbcnews.com/news/us-news/john-perry-barlow-open-internet-champion-grateful-dead-lyricist-dies-n845781

9 http://shop.oreilly.com/product/9781565929920.do

10 https://www.eff.org/about/history

11 Barlow's full declaration can be read here (love it or loathe it, it's certainly a fascinating document and an insight into a particular time and vision): https://www.eff.org/cyberspace-independence

12 https://www.eff.org/files/annual-report/2017/index.html#FinancialsModal

13 The Knight Foundation is a major US funder of journalism, technology and freedom-of-expression projects in the common interest.

14 https://panopticlick.eff.org/results?aat=1&t=111&dnt=111

15 https://www.eff.org/privacybadger

16 https://www.eff.org/https-everywhere

17 https://certbot.eff.org/

18 This is a pseudonym, but one Kidane uses in real life with his diaspora community too.

19 https://uk.kantar.com/tech/social/2018/gen-z-is-the-generation-taking-a-stand-for-privacy-on-social-media/

20 Cohn notes this line of reasoning is central to Cory Doctorow's online privacy themes in his young adult book, *Little Brother*.

21 https://www.alexa.com/siteinfo/wikipedia.org

22 https://stats.wikimedia.org/v2/#/en.wikipedia.org

23 https://en.wikipedia.org/wiki/Wikipedia:Statistics

24 https://foundation.wikimedia.org/wiki/2016-2017_Fundraising_Report

25 https://www.vogue.co.uk/article/how-the-conduit-plans-to-change-the-world

26 https://en.wikipedia.org/wiki/Bomis

27 https://en.wikipedia.org/wiki/Block_of_Wikipedia_in_Turkey

28 https://en.wikipedia.org/wiki/File:LE15_Gender_overall_in_2018.png

29 https://www.theatlantic.com/technology/archive/2015/10/how-wikipedia-is-hostile-to-women/411619/

NOTES

30 https://www.nature.com/articles/d41586-018-05947-8
31 As highlighted in a Twitter thread from Demos's Carl Miller here: https://twitter.com/carljackmiller/status/1022055586471534592
32 Zittrain is the author of *The Future of the Internet — And How To Stop It*, which is well worth a read.

CONCLUSION

1 https://www.populationpyramid.net/world/2018/
2 I was at first relatively sure I had coined this term myself, but a Google search throws up a few results, including this from Shoshana Zuboff (author of *The Age of Surveillance Capitalism*) article from 2014: https://www.shoshanazuboff.com/new/my-new-article-on-the-weapons-of-mass-detection/
3 http://www.cityam.com/273662/sainsburys-shares-crash-asda-merger-torpedoed
4 https://www.bbc.co.uk/news/business-26266689
5 https://www.theguardian.com/business/2012/jan/31/fred-goodwin-stripped-of-knighthood
6 The idea that the internet is an essential service may still be contentious to some, but consider this: the idea would have been laughable a decade ago, but now in a country like the UK it is immensely difficult to access information on utility bills and payments, taxation, social housing lists, benefit information and applications, and more, without it. That digital divide will only widen.
7 https://www.theguardian.com/technology/2017/jul/27/facebook-free-basics-developing-markets

INDEX

INDEX

INDEX

259

INDEX

INDEX

INDEX

A NOTE ON THE AUTHOR

James Ball is the Global Editor of the Bureau of Investigative Journalism and the author of multiple books, including *Post-Truth*. He has worked for BuzzFeed, the *Guardian* and the *Washington Post* and his reporting projects have won the Pulitzer Prize for public service, the Scripps Howard Prize and the British Journalism Award for investigative reporting, among others.

A NOTE ON THE TYPE

The text of this book is set in Fournier. Fournier is derived from the romain du roi, which was created towards the end of the seventeenth century from designs made by a committee of the Académie of Sciences for the exclusive use of the Imprimerie Royale. The original Fournier types were cut by the famous Paris founder Pierre Simon Fournier in about 1742. These types were some of the most influential designs of the eight and are counted among the earliest examples of the 'transitional' style of typeface. This Monotype version dates from 1924. Fournier is a light, clear face whose distinctive features are capital letters that are quite tall and bold in relation to the lower-case letters, and *decorative italics, which show the influence of the calligraphy of Fournier's time.*

We refer to the internet as abstract from reality. By doing so, we obscure where the real power lies.

The internet is a network of physical cables and connections, a web of wires enmeshing the world, linking huge data centres to one another and eventually to us all. Each is owned by someone, financed by someone, regulated by someone.

In this powerful and necessary book, James Ball sets out on a global journey into the inner workings of this system. From the computer scientists to the cable guys, the billionaire investors to the advertisers, the intelligence agents to the regulators, these are the real-life figures powering the internet and pulling the strings of our society.

Ball brilliantly shows how an invention once hailed as a democratising force has concentrated power in places it already existed – that the system, in other words, remains the same as it did before.